Cooking Outside the Pizza Box

Cooking Outside the Pizza Box

Easy Recipes for Today's College Student

by Jean Patterson
and Danae Campbell

All inquiries should be addressed to:
Barron's Educational Series, Inc.
250 Wireless Boulevard
Hauppauge, New York 11788
http://www.barronseduc.com

International Standard Book No.: 0-7641-2495-1
Library of Congress Catalog Card No.: 2003052469

Library of Congress Cataloging-in-Publication Data

Patterson, Jean, 1970–
Cooking outside the pizza box : easy recipes for today's college student / by Jean Patterson and Danae Campbell.
p. cm.
Includes index.
ISBN 0-7641-2495-1
1. Cookery. I. Campbell, Danae. II. Title.

TX652.P325 2004
641.5—dc21

2003052469

PRINTED IN CHINA
9 8 7 6 5 4 3 2

Contents

Acknowledgments

This cookbook was a pleasure to write largely because of the wonderful help and guidance we received throughout the process. We'd like to thank the talented and hard-working team at Barron's Educational Series, Inc. who brought the book to life: project editor Wendy Sleppin, copy editor Pat Connell, art director Bill Kuchler, and designer Lou Vasquez. Thanks also to artist Joanne Hus for her splendid illustrations. Warmest appreciation goes to our literary agents, Ron and Mary Lee Laitsch, for always being there to encourage and champion our efforts.

We are grateful to the family members and friends who happily volunteered to test recipes, most notably Teresa, Paul, and Anna Patterson, Pete Schelden, Laurel Baker, and Jon Bullinger. Thank you to Francisco Diaz for contributing such a catchy title, and to Sarah Carter for careful proofreading of the manuscript. Thanks also to Danielle and the folks at Sweet Daddy's Coffee Lounge in Glendora for keeping us caffeinated and for cranking out the tunes. And finally, our deepest gratitude goes to Doug Davis and Jim Campbell for their steadfast love and support . . . and for eating all of the leftovers.

Getting Started

1

If you are pressed for time, new to the kitchen, on a budget, or any combination of these, then just read on. Help is on the way.

Cooking Outside the Pizza Box offers more than 110 quick, great-tasting recipes specifically designed for busy lifestyles like your own.

How did we do it? First of all, we reduced preparation times and cut back on the number of ingredients needed for each recipe. Using fewer ingredients means less money spent at the grocery store, fewer items for you to wash, peel, and chop, less time spent in front of the stove, fewer dirty dishes to wash, and most importantly, less of a wait until *you* get to eat.

Second, we made sure that the recipes would be easy to follow, without a long list of steps or complicated preparations. You don't need any specialized knowledge or experience to cook them: Just open the book, pick a recipe, and make it. For example, if you can open a can and operate a blender, you're already equipped to make an addictive White Bean-Pesto Dip. If you tend to be a bit disaster-prone in the kitchen, check out our "Don't Let This Happen to You" tips, which tell you how to avoid the most common cooking mishaps.

Last but not least, we show that feeding yourself needn't be an expensive proposition. If you're short on cash, these affordable recipes are just what you need to resist the temptation to eat out. To learn how to save money on groceries, consult our dollar-saving "Cheap Tips," which tell you how and where to buy only as much as you need at the lowest price.

Just because you're living away from home doesn't mean you have to restrict yourself to mac-and-cheese from a box every night. Cooking on your own can be surprisingly simple, convenient, and even fun. Just turn to this cookbook created especially for busy college students—and you'll be cooking up your favorite meals before you know it.

How to Follow a Recipe

On its most basic level, a recipe is just a set of instructions—in this case, a very *simple* set of instructions. To ensure success, simply follow the directions carefully.

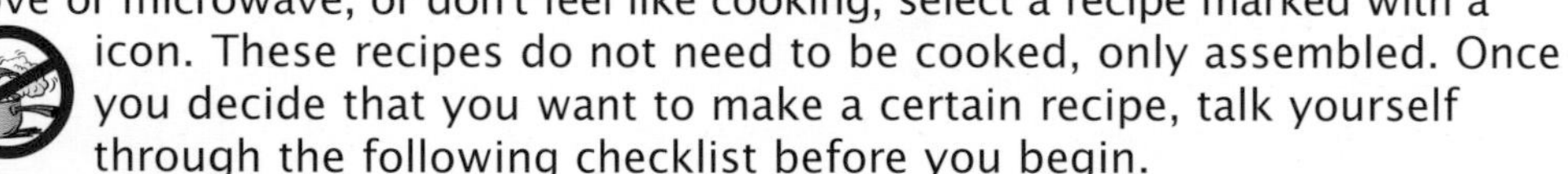

If you're in a hurry, choose a recipe marked with a icon, which means it will take 15 minutes or less to prepare and cook. If you don't have a stove or microwave, or don't feel like cooking, select a recipe marked with a icon. These recipes do not need to be cooked, only assembled. Once you decide that you want to make a certain recipe, talk yourself through the following checklist before you begin.

1. Read the recipe thoroughly at least once. Look at the ingredients section and consult your refrigerator and cupboards to see what you have on hand and what you need to buy. Check the ingredients you already have; just because you have them doesn't mean they're still usable.

2. Consider which steps need to be done ahead of time. Does the meat need to be defrosted? Does the butter need to be softened? Does the oven need to be preheated?
3. Make sure you've allotted enough time to complete the recipe. By adding the Prep Time and Cooking Time, you'll have a rough idea of how long the process will take. "Prep Time" means the amount of time it will take you to prepare the ingredients before you begin to cook or bake. This includes steps like opening cans and rinsing, peeling, and chopping ingredients.
4. Set out all of your ingredients and equipment. Having everything at your fingertips cuts down on mad dashes to the refrigerator for the next ingredient. We've designed these recipes to be prepared very quickly, but that only works if you have everything at hand. So read the recipe again, especially the steps that happen quickly one after the other. Now you're ready to begin.

How to Measure

Using the exact amounts that a recipe calls for is very important. When a recipe doesn't work out, the underlying problem often has to do with how accurately the ingredients were measured.

We've made the measuring in our recipes as easy and straightforward as possible. However, if you want to double a recipe or can't locate your 1/4-cup measure, it's a good idea to know how to convert from one type of measurement to another.

1 cup = 16 tablespoons/237 ml
1/2 cup = 8 tablespoons/118 ml
1/4 cup = 4 tablespoons/59 ml
1 tablespoon = 3 teaspoons
1/2 tablespoon = 1 1/2 teaspoons
8 ounces water = 1 cup

Measuring Dry Ingredients

To measure flour, lightly spoon it into the measuring cup and level off the top with a knife. Don't tap the measuring cup on the counter or try to pack in as much flour as you can; you'll get an inaccurate measurement. Likewise, don't measure the flour in a liquid measuring cup because you won't be able to level it off.

To measure sugar, go ahead and scoop it directly out of the bag or canister, using your measuring cup. Level off the top with a knife.

When you measure brown sugar, however, pack as much as you can into the cup to get an accurate measurement. Scoop the brown sugar in and press it down with the back of a spoon. Continue doing this until the brown sugar is level with the top of the cup.

Measuring Liquids

If you hold the liquid measuring cup in your hand while you're measuring, chances are you won't get an accurate reading. Instead, set the cup on a level surface and bend down to see if the liquid reaches the appropriate line. Don't measure liquids in dry measuring cups because they will be more likely to spill.

Measuring Small Amounts

If you're measuring teaspoons or tablespoons, you can use the same measuring spoons for both liquid and dry ingredients. Teaspoons and tablespoons should be level, not rounded.

A pinch is a very small measurement; basically, it's the amount that you can hold between the tip of your thumb and your forefinger. It's roughly 1/16 teaspoon, but there's no need to have a measuring spoon for that small an amount.

How to Use a Knife

A knife is one of the most important tools in the kitchen, and also one of the most dangerous. If you feel uneasy or unsure about handling a knife, consider taking a basic knife skills class at a local culinary school or cooking store. There you will learn basic safety principles like the following:

1. A sharp knife is a safe knife. If your knife is dull, you will tend to apply additional pressure, making the knife more liable to slip. Either buy a knife that stays sharp for a long time, or have your knife sharpened professionally. Ask at a cookware store to find out where to have your knife sharpened.
2. When carrying a knife, always hold it by the handle, with the blade facing down. When you hand a knife to another person, have them take the knife by the handle, not the blade.
3. If you happen to drop your knife, step out of the way and let it fall to the floor. Your reflexes may tell you to try to grab the knife in midair. Resist the natural temptation to do so.
4. As you cut, use your non-knife hand to hold the food, keeping your fingers tucked under. Use your knuckles to guide the knife, being careful not to scrape them. Better to loosen up on what you're holding with the non-knife hand than to risk skinning your fingers.
5. Slice with slow, even movements. Do not rush.
6. Never place a knife into a sink or dishpan full of water because someone could reach into the water and accidentally get cut. After you've cleaned a knife, place it to the side of the sink in a safe place where it won't slip into the water.

Chopping vs. Mincing

One of the most confusing things about following a recipe can be deciphering cooking terms like "chopped," "diced," and "minced." Exactly how big should the pieces be? In most cases, size is only a matter of preference, but it does affect the cooking time. When in doubt, consult the following chart for suggested sizes:

Chopped = 1/2-inch pieces
Diced = 1/4-inch pieces
Minced = 1/16-inch pieces, or as small as possible

Peeling and Mincing Garlic

Once you get the hang of it, peeling and mincing garlic is super-easy. There's no need to use bottled minced garlic or, worse yet, garlic powder. First, place a clove of garlic on the cutting board, and lay your knife flat on top of it. Using the palm of your hand, press down hard on the knife to smash the clove and split it open. The peel will loosen and slide right off. Using the blade of your knife, mince the garlic into tiny pieces.

Peeling and Chopping an Onion

Start peeling the onion by cutting off the stem end. Use your fingers to take off the peel. Next, cut the onion in half lengthwise (through the root) and place each onion half cut side down, with the root end facing you. Cut from the tip end to the root end, slicing in narrow strips up to but not through the root. Turn the onion 90 degrees clockwise, and cut narrow strips at a right angle to the first cuts. After you throw away the root end, you're left with a pile of evenly cut pieces. Repeat with the other onion half.

Cutting Fresh Herbs

Before you cut, wash the herbs well to get rid of any grit. With tougher herbs, especially rosemary or thyme, you'll want to cut or pull the leaves off the woody stems. With leafy herbs like cilantro or parsley, it's fine to eat the stems. Fold the herbs back upon themselves several times so there's less territory to cover. That way you can cut through the whole stack of herbs with each downward motion of your knife.

How to Shop for Food

Trying out a new recipe can seem daunting, especially if it has a long list of ingredients that you don't have on hand. To minimize your trips to the store and to help save you money, we've used a limited number of ingredients in our recipes. For instance, we only list a handful of common spices, such as cayenne and cinnamon, so you don't need to fill your cupboard with tiny jars that only get opened once a year.

For your convenience, we've compiled a list of these frequently used ingredients so you can have them on hand in your cupboard, fridge, or freezer. That way, when you want to try out a recipe, you'll only have a few items to pick up at the store, like fresh fruits and vegetables.

Opportunists, take note: When your parents come to town and offer to take you grocery shopping, this is the perfect list to take with you.

What to Have on Hand

Baking Items

baking soda
brown sugar (light and/or dark)
semisweet chocolate chips
unsweetened cocoa powder
cornstarch (also known as cornflour)
honey
all-purpose flour
powdered sugar (also known as icing sugar)
rolled oats (oatmeal)
sugar
pure vanilla extract

Canned Goods

beans (such as black, garbanzo, pinto)
chicken broth and/or vegetable broth
crushed tomatoes
diced tomatoes
peeled tomatoes

Dry Goods

couscous
pasta (various kinds)
rice (long-grain, basmati, and/or jasmine)

Spices

black pepper
cayenne
ground cinnamon
ground cumin
curry powder
fresh or bottled ginger
red pepper flakes
salt

Produce

garlic
onions
red onions
russet or other baking potatoes

Miscellaneous

maple syrup or pancake syrup
olive oil (not extra-virgin)
soy sauce
vegetable oil
vinegar (various kinds)

Refrigerator Items

barbecue sauce
unsalted butter
cheddar and/or jack cheese
large eggs
ketchup
mayonnaise
milk
mustard
grated or shredded Parmesan cheese (the refrigerated kind)
peanut butter
plain yogurt

Freezer Items

bacon
ground beef
boneless skinless chicken breasts
boneless skinless chicken thighs
flour tortillas
fruit (such as strawberries, blackberries, blueberries)
ice cream
nuts (such as walnuts, almonds, cashews)
ground turkey
vegetables (such as corn, peas)

Before you go to the store, take a minute to write down a shopping list to help you remember exactly what you want to buy. If you go shopping without a list, you'll be more likely to spend money on items that you don't really need.

Consider organizing your shopping list according to the various sections of the supermarket, grouping items such as dry goods, dairy, meat, and produce. That way, you won't have to go down the same aisle more than once.

Deciding Where to Shop

Your grocery budget will go much further if you figure out where to buy each item at the cheapest price. Depending on the types of stores that are located in your neighborhood, you might consider dividing your food shopping among several of them to get the most for your money. For instance, you could buy spices, rice, and pasta from the bulk section of a health-food store, where they're cheapest, but then shop for all of your other groceries at a supermarket, where you can take advantage of sale prices and coupons. Your decision about where to shop will largely depend on your own preferences and how much time you want to dedicate to finding the lowest prices.

Supermarkets

Pros: Supermarkets are everywhere, offering a wide selection of almost all the ingredients you could possibly need. For the budget-minded, supermarkets offer specials, price breaks, and club cards, and most will accept coupons as well. If you watch the newspaper ads and clip coupons, you can save a lot of money at a supermarket.

With supermarket produce, the key is to buy in season. If you happen to be shopping for produce that isn't in season, the supermarket will most likely still have it. For instance, if you simply must have fresh tomatoes or strawberries in January, you can find them at a supermarket. However, they won't taste as good as they do when they're in season.

Cons: Supermarkets have a lot of overhead, which tends to affect the prices of items that aren't on sale. And the downside to clipping coupons is that you may end up buying things that you normally wouldn't. This is fine, if the coupon helps you buy a product for next to nothing. However, you shouldn't buy something just for the sake of using up a coupon. Plus, supermarket produce is not always the freshest you can find. Some of the items have been trucked across the country and then left sitting on the shelf for a long time.

Warehouse Stores

Pros: Warehouse stores sell items in large quantities. If you have roommates or friends who are willing to chip in, you can buy food at a much cheaper rate, especially meat and frozen items. Another good bet is stocking up on household items like multi-packs of paper towels and napkins. If you're on the lookout for kitchen equipment, visit a warehouse store to get reasonable prices on blenders, toaster ovens, and coffee makers.

Cons: Not everybody wants to have a 10-pound bag of carrots in the fridge or a freezer stuffed with a 20-pack of boneless skinless chicken breasts. If you don't have a lot of extra room in your kitchen, then shopping at a warehouse store may not be the best option for you. Also, this type of store can be very crowded, especially on weekends, so be prepared to spend some time walking around and standing in line. Last but not least, some warehouse stores require a membership card, which may mean paying an annual fee. If you know someone who has a card, tag along on their next shopping trip.

Specialty Food Stores

Pros: Specialty food stores are known for selling top-quality ingredients at a reduced price. If you're looking for items like specialty cheeses, artisan breads, fish, or packaged nuts, you'll find cheaper prices at a specialty food store than you will at a supermarket. Some of these stores sell products with their own private label, which makes them less expensive than name-brand products you would find elsewhere.

Cons: Specialty food stores are only available in certain cities. We find that it's easy to get carried away in these places because we see so many things that we want but don't really need. Also, stores of this type don't have many items on sale and don't offer the types of bargains and promotions that you would find at a supermarket.

Ethnic Grocery Stores

Pros: If you like trying new or unfamiliar ingredients, then you'll enjoy shopping at ethnic grocery stores. There you'll find an interesting mix of items that would be much more expensive at a supermarket, or perhaps not sold there at all. For example, an Indian grocery store will sell spices for next to nothing, a Hispanic grocery store will offer a wide selection of fresh and dried chiles, and an Asian grocery store will sell exotic and often unfamiliar produce.

Cons: Depending on where you live, this type of store may be too far away to visit regularly. Also, you won't find a wide selection of ingredients at an ethnic grocery store—just the ones that are specific to that certain cuisine.

Health-Food Stores

Pros: Perhaps the best part of a health-food store is the bulk section. There you can buy as much or as little as you want of items like flour, rice, pasta, granola, snacks, and spices. If buying organic produce is important to you, this is the place to go. Dairy-free, soy, whole-grain, and vegetarian options are also plentiful.

Cons: Packaged items, meats, and produce can be relatively expensive at a health-food store, but you may find that the quality of the product justifies the higher price.

Farmers Markets and Roadside Stands

Pros: For the best, freshest produce you can buy, visit a farmers market or roadside produce stand. There you'll find a wide selection of tomatoes, melons, squash, berries, and other fruits and vegetables, with much better quality than you'll find elsewhere. Items like corn, plums, and strawberries are juicy and sweet like they're supposed to be because they're sold only when they're in season. And because the fruits and vegetables being sold are usually grown locally, they may have been picked the very same day that you buy them. The farmers on hand are usually very helpful and are happy to give you advice about how to select perfectly ripe produce and how to prepare it.

Cons: Farmers markets aren't open every day of the week, and may not even be open year-round, so be sure to check the market's schedule before you make the trip. Depending on where you live, the nearest farmers market may be too far away for you to visit regularly.

Farmers markets can be unpredictable, but that's part of the fun. You never know what they're going to have. All of the produce is seasonal, so you have a limited window of opportunity for buying it. Certain items that you love, like peaches, apricots, corn, or a certain type of lettuce, may only be available a few weeks out of the year, so you'll have to snatch them up when you see them. Also, because the freshness of the fruits and vegetables is better than what you'd find at a supermarket, the prices tend to be higher as well.

How to Set Up a Kitchen

Buying all the equipment that you need for a kitchen can be an expensive business. It's easy to go crazy and think you need every sort of fancy gadget that's out there. But in reality, a kitchen only needs a few crucial things; the rest is just a matter of preference.

Try to buy the best-quality equipment you can, even if that means a skillet that costs you $5 at a yard sale. That pan might end up being the best one you'll ever own, or it may just tide you over until you can buy the kind you really want.

Hand-Me-Downs

Before setting foot in a store, ask around. Do your folks have extra kitchen stuff that they don't mind loaning or giving away? Do you know someone who's moving or getting married and no longer needs some of their old kitchen equipment? Perhaps your kitchen can benefit from hand-me-downs.

Gifts

How many times has someone asked you what you would like for your birthday? Next time, instead of saying, "Oh, anything will be fine," request a new toaster oven or a blender. (Go for the big-ticket items if you can.) The giver will feel happy to give you something that you can use, and you'll be ever so pleased on the receiving end.

Garage Sales

Don't be put off by buying equipment that's already used: Someone else's reject could be exactly what you need for your kitchen. People often sell perfectly good kitchen equipment like blenders or coffee makers because they haven't been using them or because they don't match the new color scheme of their kitchen. Since you don't really need to have the latest models in your own kitchen anyway, you can benefit from their extravagance. You might even be able to talk them down to a cheaper price. (Bring cash in small bills.) Before you buy, however, make sure the equipment isn't broken or in bad shape.

Essential Items

So what exactly do you need to equip your kitchen? Here's a list of basic items that will help get you started. This list is by no means concrete; add or subtract according to your own preferences and cooking style.

All-purpose knife: A large, sharp knife will be one of the most important utensils in your kitchen. You will use this knife nearly every time you cook. Accordingly, you want one that feels comfortable in your hand and that will do the job right every time. Look for a knife with a blade that is 6 or more inches long—the longer the knife, the more you'll be able to chop at once. If possible, choose a knife that has a full "tang"—this means that the metal of the blade is actually one piece that goes all the way through the handle. You'll be able to see it when you look at the handle.

Paring knife: Although you probably won't use a paring knife as often as you will an all-purpose knife, it's nice to have one handy for smaller jobs, such as coring tomatoes or cutting the stems off strawberries. Paring knives are much smaller, about 3 to 4 inches long, and fairly cheap. Don't use a paring knife to do a job it's not cut out for, such as chopping onion or slicing meat. Get out the all-purpose knife instead.

Vegetable peeler: There's no need to buy a fancy type of vegetable peeler. Just make sure to get one that feels comfortable in your hand. The traditional swivel kind of peeler is sturdy, inexpensive, and widely available.

Cutting boards: A large wood or plastic cutting board is a vital item that will last you for several years. If you can swing it, consider getting several boards in various colors. That way, you can designate one cutting board for raw meats, one for strong, smelly foods like onions and garlic, and one for milder or sweet foods. To help a wood board last longer, do not leave it soaking in water, as it can warp and break apart at the seams.

Small and large nonstick skillets: Two skillets—also known as frying pans or sauté pans—are all that you'll need for your kitchen. There's no reason to buy an entire set with four or more different sizes: You only need a large one and a small one. And there's no reason why the two skillets have to match. Keep an eye out for sales and buy what you like. Having nonstick skillets will make your life much easier. For one thing, you won't need to use as much oil or butter in your cooking. Plus, cleaning a nonstick pan is much, much easier than cleaning a regular one. Look for skillets with heavy, thick bottoms; they heat more evenly, so your food is less likely to burn.

Small and large saucepans: Just as with skillets, your saucepans should have heavy bottoms, if possible. A 2-quart (or 2-liter) saucepan will be just the right size for most of your everyday cooking. Get a 4-quart (or 4-liter) saucepan as well for boiling pasta or making large amounts of soup. If you can get your hands on a stockpot, that would be even better.

Small, medium, and large mixing bowls: Look for a small bowl that holds 1 quart or 1 liter, a medium one that holds about twice that, plus a really big one. Any type of bowl will work—plastic, tempered glass, glass, metal, or stoneware. Often, bowls can be purchased more cheaply as a set. (Of course, they don't have to match to work.)

Measuring cups and spoons: You will use your measuring cups and spoons constantly, so make sure to get a kind that you like. Either plastic or metal is fine. For measuring spoons, you need to have at least the following: 1/4 teaspoon, 1/2 teaspoon, 1 teaspoon, and 1 tablespoon. For measuring cups, you will need 1/4 cup, 1/3 cup, 1/2 cup, and 1 cup. Some sets come with extra measuring cups, such as 3/4 cup or 2/3 cup, but you don't really need them. If adding fractions gave you nightmares in elementary school, however, then maybe you should spring for the extra measuring cups.

Liquid measuring cup: The typical size for a liquid measuring cup is a 1- or 2-cup (237 ml or 473 ml) measure. Either one will do. We recommend getting a liquid measuring cup made of tempered glass so you can use it in the microwave to heat up water or milk.

Rubber spatula: Rubber spatulas come in fun colors, but of course a plain white one will also do the job. Make sure the spatula says "heatproof," or else it may burn in your skillet. Rubber spatulas are especially useful for mixing batter, scraping out blenders and mixing bowls, and scrambling eggs.

Wooden or large spoon: Keep a large spoon next to the stove for all of those times when you need to give something a stir. Wooden spoons are especially nice because they don't scratch nonstick pans. With other kinds of pans, you can use a metal spoon instead, if you prefer.

Pancake turner: Pancake turners come in various sizes; it's best to get a wide one, so you'll be able to use it for flipping French toast, meat, and, of course, pancakes. Pancake turners are usually made of plastic, with or without slits. If your skillet is nonstick, do not use a metal pancake turner; it will damage the pan's surface.

Tongs: Once you have a set of tongs, you'll use them for all sorts of things, like flipping over meat and tossing salads. Get the tongs that look like long tweezers, not the plastic ones with scissor-like handles (you'll know them when you see them). If you don't have tongs, just use two forks.

Blender: When it comes to blenders, there's no need to get one with a bunch of power settings: High and low speeds are all you will use anyway. Just make sure the blender has a wattage of at least 450. Blenders are often sold at thrift stores and garage sales. As with any electrical appliance, if you get a used one, plug it in and see if it works before you buy it. Also, check to make sure that the blender has a lid and that the jar isn't cracked. The blender jar can be made of either plastic or glass. Glass is heavier and has the potential to break, but plastic can warp if it gets too hot in the dishwasher.

Toaster: Either a slot toaster or a toaster oven will come in very handy in your kitchen. Toaster ovens are more expensive and take up more space, but they're also more versatile: You can use them to toast bagels or large or thick slices of bread, or to heat up French bread pizzas and frozen French fries.

Baking sheet: A baking sheet, also known as a cookie sheet or a sheet pan, is a flat metal sheet, with or without sides, that can be used for tasks like baking cookies or toasting nuts in the oven. There's no need to buy an expensive one, but it should not be flimsy. You don't want the baking sheet to warp or buckle as it heats up in the oven. Baking sheets come in various sizes, so make sure that the one you're planning to buy is small enough to fit inside your oven.

Dish towels/pot holders: Dish towels are important to get; pot holders are optional. Either one will protect your hands from heat when you're handling hot dishes or moving items in or out of the oven. Oven mitts are not necessary unless you're paranoid about burning yourself. We like to have at least four dish towels on hand. That way, there are at least two clean towels in the kitchen at all times: one to dry dishes, and one to handle hot dishes. Just make sure you don't use a wet dish towel to handle a hot dish; the water will conduct the heat, making the dish towel very hot.

Grater: An all-purpose, four-sided box grater—the kind with the handle on top—is the best kind of grater to have around because you can do so much with it: grate, shred, and even slice. You'll be using the largest holes of the grater the most often, for shredding ingredients like cheese and carrots. Watch out for your knuckles when you're shredding and grating; it's easy to get carried away and scrape your skin instead of the food.

Colander: When you're shopping for a colander, think: Bigger is better. For tasks like draining pasta, you want a colander that's as big as a large bowl but that doesn't have such big holes in the bottom that spaghetti slips through them. Some colanders come with handles, others don't. You don't really need them. Colanders come in either metal or plastic; go with your own preference.

Can opener: There's no need to buy an electric can opener; it will just take up space on your countertop. Instead, get the old-fashioned, nonelectric, twisty kind. Usually they incorporate a bottle opener as well.

Large ovenproof baking dish: If you want to make pot roast or roast chicken, you'll need a large baking dish that's at least 4 inches deep. The shape doesn't really matter; it can be rectangular, round, or oval. And if the dish comes with a lid, that's nice, too.

Square baking dish: If you want to bake brownies or chocolate cake, a 9-inch baking dish is just the right size to have. The dish can be made of glass, metal, or earthenware; it's your preference.

Aluminum foil: You'll use aluminum foil over and over again in the kitchen, for tasks like keeping food warm, covering a saucepan or skillet, or lining baking dishes to make them easier to clean. Compare the prices for smaller and larger rolls; you'll often get much more for your money by buying a larger roll. Plus, you won't run out of foil for a long time.

Metal basket steamer: A basket steamer is only essential if you're a big fan of steamed vegetables and don't have a microwave. This type of steamer opens up like a flower and has lots of small holes that let the steam pass through.

Items That Are Nice to Have

Cooling rack: A wire cooling rack allows air to circulate underneath a hot baking dish so that the dish cools down. The rack also protects the kitchen counter from heat. If you don't have a cooling rack, just set the hot baking dish on the stovetop.

Pie plate: There's no need to go out and buy a pie plate; someone you know probably has a cheap disposable aluminum one that they will be happy to give to you. If you're buying a frozen pie crust, it already comes with a disposable plate that you can use over and over again—that is, if you don't accidentally stab a hole through it when you're cutting the pie.

Whisk: A whisk comes in handy when you're mixing cake batter or scrambling lots of eggs. Flimsy whisks are fairly cheap, but it's better to buy a sturdier one, especially if you plan to use it a lot. Look for a medium-sized whisk made of either stainless steel or plastic.

Bread knife: If you buy bagels or big, crusty loaves of unsliced bread, it's nice to have a serrated knife. This will be a fairly long knife, with tiny teeth that easily cut through the bread without squishing it.

Know Your Appliances

As you gain more experience in the kitchen, you'll get a feel for your appliances and their individual quirks. Ovens, stoves, and microwaves vary widely in temperature, so you may have to adjust the times and temperature levels listed in the recipes for your specific appliances.

Stove: If you have an electric stove, heat levels like "low" and "medium" are listed right on the dial. Even so, these settings are not set in stone; pay attention to see if you need to increase or decrease the heat. Likewise, if you have a gas stove that puts out a big flame, adjust the recipe instructions accordingly. Our version of "medium" may be closer to "medium-low" on your stove.

Oven: Does your oven have a thermometer inside? If so, look at it when the oven is on to see if the actual temperature in the oven matches the temperature on the oven dial. If your oven runs too hot, you may need to adjust the dial to a lower temperature than the recipe says. Similarly, if your oven is hotter on one side than it is on the other (electric ovens are notorious for this), you may need to turn the baking dish around halfway through the baking process.

Microwave: Microwaves vary widely in wattage, so the cooking times listed in a recipe may be very different from what your microwave will do. In most cases, we tell you to stop the microwave periodically to check on the dish. If your microwave doesn't have a turntable (most do), you'll need to turn the dish around every once in a while to help the food cook evenly. You most likely already know this, but we'll mention it just in case: No metal in the microwave. This includes the wires on a Chinese takeout box, aluminum foil, and dishes with metal trim.

How to Clean Up

Whenever you cook, there's bound to be some kind of cleanup involved. This may not be your favorite part of the process, but it's necessary if you want to have clean dishes the next time you cook.

The best time to clean a dish or pan is right after you use it. Even if you're not in the mood, it's important to tackle this task right away, before the food dries out and gets really stuck. If you can't wash the dishes right away, at least rinse off the larger pieces of food and soak the dishes in hot, soapy water until you can get to them.

With the following items on hand, you can make short work of dirty dishes.

Dishwashing liquid: Buy a large bottle of dishwashing liquid if you can, because it tends to get used up quickly. Check the instructions on the bottle: Some products are more concentrated than others, so you may only need to use a small amount to do the job.

Baking soda: Among its many talents, baking soda makes a safe, gentle scrub for dishes. Sprinkle baking soda on the dish that you want to clean, add a little bit of water to make a paste, and scrub. Baking soda can also be used to scrub your kitchen sink.

Sponge: We like to use the sponges that have two textures: one side smooth, the other side rough. This kind of sponge does double duty, as the rough side can help you with the more difficult messes. Don't leave the sponge soaking in water once you're done using it; instead, let it dry out in between uses. Once a week or so, microwave the sponge for 10 seconds to kill bacteria. Replace the sponge every two months, or whenever it starts looking shaggy.

Scrubbing brush: A scrubbing brush with a long handle is perfect for cleaning out tall glasses and jars. It's also good for especially sticky or gooey cleanup jobs; a mess that would otherwise muck up your sponge will easily wash off the bristles of the brush. If you have a dishwasher, clean the scrubbing brush by running it through the cycle with the other dishes.

Scouring pad: For really difficult cleaning jobs, you may need to invest in a scouring pad. Be careful not to use one on nonstick surfaces because it will scratch them.

Dish towels: You'll want to have a lot of dish towels on hand for drying dishes, especially if you don't have a dishwasher. Wash the towels before you use them for the first time, to get rid of any lint or dust.

Drying rack: If you're washing dishes by hand, you'll need some kind of rack to dry them on. You can choose between a folding rack, made of either wood or metal, or a plastic dish rack. The plastic kind takes up more counter space but can hold a lot of dishes at one time. The collapsible drying rack looks a bit spiffier and can be folded and put away when you're not using it.

Using the Dishwasher

With some dishwashers, you need to pre-rinse the dishes to make sure they come clean. Give each dish a quick rinse to get most of the food off.

Don't load the dishwasher haphazardly. Make sure there is empty space around each dish so that the water and detergent can get to it. Place utensils eating surfaces up, handles down, so that they will get thoroughly cleaned. Lighter items like plastic containers tend to move around during the cycle, sometimes collecting big pools of water, so watch out for spillage as you open the dishwasher.

If you run out of dishwasher detergent, don't be tempted to use the kind of dishwashing liquid that's used for washing dishes by hand. It won't work right and could damage the dishwasher.

If you have hard water, you could also use a rinse agent like Jet-Dry, which will help to prevent water spots on glasses.

How to Clean the Blender

Cleaning a blender is super easy, as long as you do it right away. Fill the blender jar half full with warm water, replace the lid, and give the blender a few whirs. Sponge out any leftover bits of food.

For a more thorough cleaning, when the blender seems especially dirty, take the blender jar apart. (Yes, you *can* take it apart.) Unscrew the base and separate the blade, washer, and base from the jar of the blender. Give the pieces a good scrub, let them dry in a safe place (be careful where you put the blade), and put the blender back together again.

How to Clean the Microwave

The best time to clean a microwave is right after you've messed it up. With pasta sauce splattered all over the walls or melted cheese stuck to the turntable, it can get pretty ugly in there. The longer you wait to clean, the more cooked on the food will get.

The turntable is easy to clean, since you can take it out and wash it by hand or possibly in the dishwasher. The hard part is those stubborn bits of food stuck to the sides of the microwave. Use steam to loosen them by boiling water in the microwave in a mug or other microwave-safe container. Next, clean the inside of the microwave with a two-sided sponge, using a scouring pad for the toughest spots. Baking soda paste would work well, as would an all-purpose kitchen cleaner.

How to Clean the Fridge and Freezer

Cleaning the refrigerator can be a big chore, especially if you don't do it regularly. But once you're done, the refrigerator will have a lot more space and a much better smell.

First priority: Get rid of the food that's no longer edible. Get out a big trash bag; you're going to need it for all of those out-of-date milk cartons, moldy leftovers, shriveled produce, and slimy greens. Check the expiration dates and don't take any chances. When in doubt, throw it out.

Don't forget the freezer. If something has so much ice stuck to it that you can't identify it, toss it. Frozen food does go bad eventually, and freezer burn makes food taste nasty. You may have had good intentions to cook the food that you put in there, but it's time to let go.

Take a good look at what's left inside, especially those jarred condiments that you've had for ages. Are you really going to use that jar of mustard with only a thin crusty layer left? What about that jar of capers that you opened once and never again? In the interest of making space, assess what you will actually use, and get rid of what you won't. You can always buy it again.

Be careful that you don't accidentally throw away any of your roommate's food. However, if you find a mystery container and no one knows how it got there or who owns it, it's time to junk it.

If your fridge is not that dirty inside, use a moistened sponge or paper towel and an all-purpose kitchen cleanser to wipe down all of the surfaces. If there are stuck-on messes, however, you may need to disassemble the fridge and wash all of the shelves, racks, and drawers by hand. The freezer is probably not as dirty inside, but it can accumulate drips and bits of food that need to be cleaned.

Now that your fridge is nice and clean and fresh smelling, put an open box of baking soda inside to keep it odor-free. The same goes for the freezer. Baking soda will help keep your ice cubes from tasting like something other than ice.

How to Be Safe in the Kitchen

Kitchen accidents can usually be prevented if you pay careful attention to what you're doing and avoid taking unnecessary risks. For instance, you'd never guess how hot a pot handle can get until you touch one by mistake. We've burned our palms by grabbing hot handles, and believe us, it'll ruin your whole day. To prevent this from happening, once the pot is off the flame, place a dish towel over the handle to remind yourself (and alert others) that it's hot.

Here are some more guidelines to help you stay out of harm's way:

- Always turn pot handles toward the back of the stove. Otherwise, someone could accidentally bump the saucepan and spill its contents over themselves and the floor. Or, if there are children around, they could pull the saucepan down on top of themselves.
- If someone else is with you, and you're in a small kitchen with not much room to maneuver, you may bump into each other. Add a sharp knife or a pot of boiling water to this scene, and you could have a dangerous collision. One of the best things you can do is let that other person know when you are behind them. As you pass by, say "Behind you" loud enough for them to hear.
- Likewise, if you are carrying a very hot item through the kitchen, say

"Hot" loud enough to alert everyone else. That way, they will give you plenty of room to get to where you need to go.

- Always alert others to dangers they may be unaware of, such as a slippery wet spot on the floor. Better yet, just clean it up right away.
- Never leave sharp or breakable items such as knives or glassware sitting in a sink or dish tub full of water, where they will be invisible. They pose a risk to anyone who's reaching down into the water.
- Look inside the oven before you turn it on. In kitchens that have limited cupboard space, people tend to store things in the oven. This is fine to do, as long as all of the items are oven-safe. Even so, it can be a lot of trouble to move a bunch of items out of the oven once they're already hot.
- Last but not least, always use the safety devices on kitchen equipment, such as the lid on a blender.

What to Wear

Your choice of clothing can help protect you from the heat of the stove or oven. If you're frying something on the stove, for example, wear a long-sleeved shirt to protect your arms from spattering oil. When you're washing dishes, however, it's nice to be able to roll up your sleeves and not get them wet.

Depending on what you're wearing, you may want to put on an apron to protect your clothing. If you're already in your grubbies, no worries.

To be perfectly safe, shoes should be nonskid, closed toe, and comfortable. We know there will be times when you feel like cooking barefoot or in your slippers. If something falls to the floor, such as boiling water, a heavy pan, or a sharp knife, you'll be better off with some kind of protection.

If you have long hair, pull it back away from your face for your own safety and to keep it out of the food.

Basic First Aid

Even if you are being very careful, accidents do happen. If you get a serious burn, one in which the skin is blistered or broken, call your doctor. For minor burns, run cold water over the skin (avoid hot water, as it will intensify the burning sensation). First-aid burn cream or spray analgesic will also help to alleviate the pain of minor burns.

If you get a serious cut that won't stop bleeding or looks like it may require stitches, go to the emergency room. If it's a minor cut, wash it well with soap and water and apply pressure with a clean towel to stop the bleeding. If you're not finished cooking, make sure the cut is well covered in order to protect yourself and the food.

Food Safety

Food poisoning is awful enough when you get it from restaurant food, but it's especially infuriating when you have only yourself to blame. The following tips will help you eliminate many of the germs that can cause food poisoning.

- For obvious reasons, always wash your hands before handling food or any kitchen equipment.
- If you can afford to have more than one cutting board, do. Designate a cutting board for raw meat only and be very diligent about cleaning it.
- After you use your knife to cut raw meat, wash it well before cutting any other ingredients.
- Once a month or so, disinfect your cutting boards and other kitchen surfaces with a solution of 1/2 teaspoon bleach and 2 quarts or 2 liters of water. Fill a spray bottle with this mixture and use it to clean your cutting boards, stovetop, counter, sink, and other surfaces. Or combine the bleach solution in a bowl and apply with a sponge.
- Keep perishable items like meat, dairy, seafood, and eggs refrigerated at all times. When you get home from the grocery store, put those items in the refrigerator right away. Likewise, once you take them out of the refrigerator, put them back as soon as you've used them. Don't leave them setting on the counter for more than a few minutes at a time. If you're one of those people who tend to leave the milk out on the counter while you're eating your breakfast, the milk is going to go bad much faster, possibly even before the expiration date.

Expiration Dates

Expiration dates are very helpful, but you can't always trust them. Some items last longer than their expiration dates, whereas some go bad sooner. When in doubt, follow your nose. Smell the milk before you pour it: if it smells funky, it probably is. Better to throw it away than ruin your whole dish.

Always check the expiration dates of eggs, milk, yogurt, and meat before you buy them. Sometimes you can get a better price on meat that's nearing its expiration date. This is fine, as long as you cook or freeze the meat right away.

The Safe Way to Defrost

To defrost small items like frozen shrimp or vegetables, place them in a colander and rinse with cool water. Refrigerate or use right away.

For larger items, defrost in the refrigerator. The bigger the item, the longer it will take to thaw. If you're defrosting a whole chicken, give it at least two days, placing it in the coldest part of the refrigerator.

Never defrost a frozen item by setting it out on the counter at room temperature. You may remember your mom defrosting the Thanksgiving turkey by leaving it out overnight. This is a major no-no. Yes, you survived, but it's best not to tempt fate.

Most microwaves have a "defrost" setting, which is much faster than defrosting in the refrigerator. However, the microwave can defrost unevenly, meaning that the meat ends up getting cooked on the edges.

Storing Leftovers

Hot food should not go in the refrigerator until it's had a chance to cool down. Otherwise, it will raise the temperature of the nearby items in the refrigerator. To help the hot food cool faster, keep it uncovered. If you can transfer it to one or more large, shallow containers, all the better. With soups, it also helps to stir every 10 minutes or so to let some of the residual heat out.

Of course, leaving food out on the counter for too long can also be unsafe. If you have a big pot that you need to cool down quickly, place it in the sink and surround it with ice and cold water to help the process go faster.

Once you've had leftovers in the refrigerator for a few days, you may wonder if they're still safe to eat. Leftover vegetables may not be as tasty, but they probably won't hurt you. However, leftovers that contain meat or dairy products should be thrown away after two to three days.

When you freeze leftovers, use a freezer bag rather than a regular plastic bag, which doesn't offer enough protection. Label the freezer bag with that day's date and the bag's contents. It's amazing how much lentil soup can resemble pot roast if it's left in the freezer for too long.

How to Share a Kitchen

Every roommate has different cleaning standards, and unfortunately, these tend to be most obvious in the kitchen. Before you know it, a major blowup can happen over a seemingly minor thing. Just as married couples may squabble about how to squeeze the toothpaste tube, a roommate may disapprove if someone uses the same knife to scoop out both the peanut butter and the jelly, thereby getting bits of peanut butter in the jelly or vice versa. Finding toast crumbs in the butter is another common pet peeve.

Get these issues out in the open as soon as you can, before anyone starts to feel upset. Be flexible and willing to make compromises. For example, don't expect everyone else to load the dishwasher the way that you do, even if it does seem like the best way.

The following questions are meant to help you talk with your roommates about how to share the kitchen. Once you have a clear set of guidelines and expectations, hold yourself to them.

- Does everyone have their own designated shelf space in the cupboards and fridge, or is it a free-for-all? The best strategy for a small kitchen, we believe, is to allot an equal amount of space for each person. Otherwise, there's a chance that your roommates will give you the cold shoulder because your ice cream stash is taking up all of the freezer space.
- Do you and your roommates share some or all of your ingredients? For pantry items like flour, sugar, vegetable oil, and spices, it makes sense to share ingredients (splitting the cost), rather than having each roommate buy one of everything. Maybe you only want to share ingredients

on an occasional basis. That's fine, too. If you use someone else's ingredient, try to replace it right away. Otherwise, a week or so later, when they want to make chocolate-chip cookies, for example, they'll get halfway through the recipe only to find that the chocolate chips have disappeared.

- Do you share pots and pans, dishes, silverware, and/or plastic containers? The nice thing about sharing is that you won't have to buy as much equipment for the kitchen. But sharing has its downside, too. Once your stuff merges, it's easy to forget whose items are whose. Someone could accidentally break your favorite mug or cereal bowl, or just not wash it out before you want to use it. If you don't want anyone else using your dishes, hiding them under your bed seems a bit silly (we know several people who have done this, just to avoid a confrontation). Better to have a clear understanding from the very beginning.
- Do you split some or all of the grocery costs? Let's say you decide to buy certain staples together, such as milk or butter. This is an especially good idea when you can get a price break by buying in larger quantities. When you share a grocery bill in this way, it's only fair to make sure that all of the items you buy together are actually eaten by everyone who made a contribution. If there's a certain item that only you want, best to pay for it by yourself.
- Do you take turns cooking for each other, or does everyone fend for themselves? If your kitchen is especially small, it probably doesn't work to have more than one person cooking at the same time. One solution is to have one person cook dinner, and then have everyone else clean up. If you and your roommates have very different tastes or diets, however, sharing the cooking responsibilities probably won't work. And if cooking is new to you, you may not want to offer to cook for someone else until you have more experience under your belt.
- What's the longest amount of time that dirty dishes are allowed to sit in the sink or on the counter? Agree to a reasonable time limit, and hold yourself to it. Every now and again, it's all right to wash a roommate's dirty dishes. But if you do it too often, you may be setting a bad precedent for yourself. It's no fun to start cooking only to realize that the pan you want to use has a four-day-old crust of scrambled eggs on it. Better to gently remind your roommate about the agreed-upon time limit, and have them wash their own dishes.
- Do you take turns cleaning, or do you assign chores, like cleaning the stove, sink, and floor? How often do you take out the trash and recycling? When everyone has a busy schedule, chores tend to get neglected until one person just can't stand the mess any longer. Better to designate a weekly or monthly cleaning time when everyone can pitch in; that way, no one feels like they're doing more than their share of the work.

Special Menus

Romantic Menu

Tomato, Mozzarella, and Basil Salad / 124
Roasted Whole Chicken with Lemon and Herbs / 80–81
Asparagus with Browned Butter / 116
purchased French bread with butter
Chocolate-Covered Strawberries / 137

Cooking for a Crowd

Basic Green Salad / 117
Spicy Chili / 101
purchased cornbread
The Very Best Chocolate Chip Bar Cookies / 130–131

Holiday Menu

Sugar & Spice Nuts / 38
Roasted Turkey Breast with Cranberry-Orange Sauce / 82–83
Garlic Mashed Potatoes / 112–113
Buttery Glazed Carrots / 111
Green Beans with Almonds / 115
Easy Pumpkin Pie / 140

Picnic Menu

Garlicky Hummus with vegetables for dipping / 34
Roasted Turkey Breast (sliced and made into sandwiches) / 82
Couscous and Vegetable Salad / 126
Walnut Chunk Brownies / 132–133

Summer Fun Menu

Perfect Corn on the Cob / 110
Old-Fashioned Hamburgers with the Works / 60–61
Chunky Potato Salad and/or Classic Coleslaw / 121–122
Ice cream sundaes with Dark Chocolate Sauce and
Hot Caramel Sauce / 128–129

Movie Night Menu

Popcorn Flavor Mixes (Pizza and/or Garlic Lovers') / 40
Barbecue Chicken Pizza / 67
Caesar Salad with Garlic Croutons / 118
Strawberries with Sour Cream and Brown Sugar / 136

Asian Menu

Pan-Fried Asian Dumplings with Dipping Sauce / 91
Teriyaki Chicken Breasts / 72
Basic Rice / 92
Steamed Broccoli / 109
fresh fruit

Indian Menu

Indian Chicken Curry / 73
Rice Pilaf with Cashews and Green Onion / 94
Green Beans with Almonds / 115
fresh or jarred mango slices

Italian Menu

Garlic Toasts with Tomatoes and Fresh Basil / 37
Sautéed Chicken Breasts / 71
Pasta with Homemade Pesto / 85, 87
Basic Green Salad / 117
purchased biscotti

Tex-Mex Menu

Chunky Guacamole / 35
Fresh Tomato Salsa / 36
tortilla chips
Skirt Steak Fajitas / 68–69
fresh pineapple

Vegan Menu (no meat, eggs, or dairy)

Garlicky Hummus with pita wedges and vegetables / 34
Asian Noodles with Spicy Peanut Sauce / 89–90
Basic Green Salad / 117
Chocolate-Covered Strawberries (use dairy-free chocolate) / 137

Recipes by Category

Super-Fast (15 Minutes or Less)

Look for recipes marked with the  icon.

Munchies chapter:

all recipes

Breakfast chapter:

Foolproof Fried Eggs / 42
Eggs Sunny-Side Up / 42
Scrambled Eggs / 43
Skillet-Cooked Bacon / 50
Microwave Bacon / 50
Strawberry-Yogurt Smoothie / 51
Fresh Strawberry-Yogurt Smoothie / 51
Banana-Honey Smoothie / 52
Bagels with Cream Cheese Schmears / 53

Main Courses chapter:

The Ultimate Grilled Cheese Sandwich / 57
Fancy Grilled Cheese Sandwich / 57
Cheese Quesadilla / 58
Ham and Cheese Quesadilla / 58
Basic Steak / 76–77

Pasta and Rice chapter:

The Easiest, Quickest Couscous / 95
Couscous with Peas and Parmesan / 96

Soups chapter:

Asian Dumpling Soup / 99
Asian Dumpling Soup with Chicken or Shrimp / 99–100
Cucumber-Buttermilk Soup / 106

Veggies and Salads chapter:

Stuffed Potato with Chili and Cheese / 114
Stuffed Potato with Chive Cream Cheese / 114
Basic Green Salad / 117
Greek Salad / 120
Classic Coleslaw / 121

Cucumber-Buttermilk Salad / 123
Tomato, Mozzarella, and Basil Salad / 124

Desserts chapter:

Dark Chocolate Sauce / 128
Stovetop Dark Chocolate Sauce / 128
Hot Caramel Sauce / 129
Stovetop Hot Caramel Sauce / 129
Chocolate Frosting / 135
Strawberries with Sour Cream and Brown Sugar / 136

No Cooking Required

Look for recipes marked with the  icon.

Munchies chapter:

White Bean-Pesto Dip (without Pita Crisps) / 33
Garlicky Hummus / 34
Chunky Guacamole / 35
Fresh Tomato Salsa / 36

Breakfast chapter:

Strawberry-Yogurt Smoothie / 51
Fresh Strawberry-Yogurt Smoothie / 51
Banana-Honey Smoothie / 52
Bagels with Cream Cheese Schmears / 53

Pasta and Rice chapter:

Homemade Pesto / 87
The Easiest Couscous / 95

Soups chapter:

Cucumber-Buttermilk Soup / 106
Chilled Gazpacho / 107

Veggies and Salads chapter:

Basic Green Salad / 117
Greek Salad / 120
Classic Coleslaw / 121
Cucumber-Buttermilk Salad / 123
Tomato, Mozzarella, and Basil Salad / 124

Desserts chapter:

Strawberries with Sour Cream and Brown Sugar / 136

Microwave-Friendly

Munchies chapter:

Popcorn Flavor Mixes / 40

Breakfast chapter:

Microwave Bacon / 50

Pasta and Rice chapter:

The Easiest, Quickest Couscous / 95
Couscous with Peas and Parmesan / 96

Veggies and Salads chapter:

Steamed Vegetables / 109
Stuffed Potato with Chili and Cheese / 114
Stuffed Potato with Chive Cream Cheese / 114
Microwave Mashed Potatoes / 112–113
Couscous and Vegetable Salad / 126

Desserts chapter:

Dark Chocolate Sauce / 128
Hot Caramel Sauce / 129
Microwave Chocolate Frosting / 135
Chocolate-Covered Strawberries / 137

Vegan (no meat, eggs, or dairy)

Munchies chapter:

Garlicky Hummus / 34
Chunky Guacamole / 35
Fresh Tomato Salsa / 36
Garlic Toasts with Tomatoes and Fresh Basil / 37

Breakfast chapter:

Vegan Tofu Scramble / 45

Vegetarian

Munchies chapter:

all recipes

Breakfast chapter:

all recipes except for Bacon

Main Courses chapter:

The Ultimate Grilled Cheese Sandwich / 57
Cheese Quesadilla / 58
Barbecue Tofu Burgers / 62
Portobello Mushroom Wraps with Garlic Mayonnaise / 63–64
Portobello Mushroom Wraps with Cheese / 63–64
Portobello Mushroom Wraps with Pesto / 63–64
Indian Potato and Cauliflower Curry / 65
Cranberry-Orange Sauce / 83

Pasta and Rice chapter:

Basic Pasta / 85
Homemade Pesto / 87
Fettuccine Alfredo / 88
Asian Noodles with Spicy Peanut Sauce / 89–90
Pan-Fried Asian Dumplings with Dipping Sauce
(use vegetable dumplings) / 91
Basic Rice / 92
Vegetarian Black Beans and Rice / 93
Rice Pilaf with Cashews and Green Onion / 94
Nutty Rice Pilaf / 94
The Easiest Couscous / 95
Couscous with Peas and Parmesan / 96

Soups chapter:

Vegetarian Black Bean Soup / 102–103
Vegetarian Lentil Soup / 104
Cucumber-Buttermilk Soup / 106
Chilled Gazpacho / 107

Veggies and Salads chapter:

all recipes except for Classic Spinach Salad with Warm Bacon Dressing and Stuffed Potato with Chili and Cheese

Desserts chapter:

all recipes

Freezer-Friendly

Munchies chapter:

Sugar & Spice Nuts / 38

Breakfast chapter:

Weekend-Morning French Toast / 46–47
Fluffy Buttermilk Pancakes / 48–49
Blueberry Pancakes / 48–49
Chocolate Chip Pancakes / 48–49

Coconut Pancakes / 48–49
Corn Pancakes / 48–49

Main Courses chapter:

Pot Roast with Onions, Potatoes, and Carrots / 78–79
Cranberry-Orange Sauce / 83

Pasta and Rice chapter:

Pasta Sauce with Turkey Meatballs / 86
Basic Rice / 92
Black Beans and Rice / 93
Vegetarian Black Beans and Rice / 93

Soups chapter:

Comforting Chicken Soup / 98
Comforting Chicken Soup with Rice / 98
Comforting Chicken Soup with Noodles / 98
Spicy Chili / 101
Hearty Black Bean Soup / 102–103
Vegetarian Black Bean Soup / 102–103
Lentil and Smoked Sausage Soup / 104
Vegetarian Lentil Soup / 104

Veggies and Salads chapter:

Garlic Butter / 110
Chili-Lime Butter / 110

Desserts chapter:

The Very Best Chocolate Chip Cookies / 130–131
The Very Best Chocolate Chip Bar Cookies / 130–131
Walnut Chunk Brownies / 132–133
Rich Chocolate Cake with Chocolate Frosting / 134–135
Apple Crisp / 138–139
Berry Crisp / 138–139

Fit for Company

Munchies chapter:

Garlic Toasts with Tomatoes and Fresh Basil / 37
Sugar & Spice Nuts / 38

Breakfast chapter:

Weekend-Morning French Toast with toppings / 46–47
Fluffy Buttermilk Pancakes / 48

Blueberry Pancakes / 48–49
Chocolate Chip Pancakes / 48–49
Coconut Pancakes / 48–49
Corn Pancakes / 48–49
Quick and Easy Cinnamon Crescent Rolls / 54
Chocolate-Filled Crescent Rolls / 54–55
Cheesy-Garlic Crescent Rolls / 54–55

Main Courses chapter:

Indian Potato and Cauliflower Curry / 65
Barbecue Shrimp Pizza / 67
Barbecue Chicken Pizza / 67
Sautéed Salmon with Lemon / 70
Sautéed Chicken Breasts / 71
Teriyaki Chicken Breasts / 72
Indian Chicken Curry / 73
Chicken Curry Drumsticks / 73
Crispy Turkey Cutlets / 74
Pork Chops with Sautéed Apples and Onions / 75
Basic Steak / 76–77
Pot Roast with Onions, Potatoes, and Carrots / 78–79
Roasted Whole Chicken with Lemon and Herbs / 80–81
Roasted Turkey Breast with Cranberry-Orange Sauce / 82–83

Pasta and Rice chapter:

Pasta Sauce with Turkey Meatballs / 86
Homemade Pesto / 87
Fettuccine Alfredo / 88
Asian Noodles with Spicy Peanut Sauce / 89–90

Soups chapter:

all recipes

Veggies and Salads chapter:

Buttery Glazed Carrots / 111
Mashed Potatoes / 112–113
Extra-Rich Mashed Potatoes / 112–113
Garlic Mashed Potatoes / 112–113
Green Beans with Almonds / 115
Asparagus with Browned Butter / 116
Classic Spinach Salad with Warm Bacon Dressing / 119
Tomato, Mozzarella, and Basil Salad / 124

Desserts chapter:

all recipes

Good for Winter

Munchies chapter:

Sugar & Spice Nuts / 38

Breakfast chapter:

Egg-and-Cheese Breakfast Burrito / 44
Easy Tofu Scramble / 45
Weekend-Morning French Toast / 46–47
Quick and Easy Cinnamon Crescent Rolls / 54
Chocolate-Filled Crescent Rolls / 54–55
Cheesy-Garlic Crescent Rolls / 54–55

Main Courses chapter:

Indian Potato and Cauliflower Curry / 65
Indian Chicken Curry / 73
Chicken Curry Drumsticks / 73
Crispy Turkey Cutlets / 74
Pork Chops with Sautéed Apples and Onions / 75
Pot Roast with Onions, Potatoes, and Carrots / 78–79
Roasted Whole Chicken with Lemon and Herbs / 80–81
Roasted Turkey Breast with Cranberry-Orange Sauce / 82–83

Pasta and Rice chapter:

Pasta Sauce with Turkey Meatballs / 86
Fettuccine Alfredo / 88
Black Beans and Rice / 93

Soups chapter:

Comforting Chicken Soup / 98
Comforting Chicken Soup with Rice / 98
Comforting Chicken Soup with Noodles / 98
Asian Dumpling Soup / 99–100
Spicy Chili / 101
Hearty Black Bean Soup / 102–103
Vegetarian Black Bean Soup / 102–103
Lentil and Smoked Sausage Soup / 104
Vegetarian Lentil Soup / 104
Creamy Corn and Potato Soup / 105

Veggies and Salads chapter:

Buttery Glazed Carrots / 111
Stuffed Potato with Chili and Cheese / 114
Mashed Potatoes / 112

Extra-Rich Mashed Potatoes / 112–113
Garlic Mashed Potatoes / 112–113
Spinach Salad with Warm Bacon Dressing / 119

Desserts chapter:

Dark Chocolate Sauce (over cake) / 128
Hot Caramel Sauce (over cake) / 129
Walnut Chunk Brownies / 132–133
Apple Crisp / 138–139
Berry Crisp / 138–139
Easy Pumpkin Pie / 140

Good for Summer

Munchies chapter:

White Bean-Pesto Dip with unbaked pita wedges / 33
Garlicky Hummus / 34
Chunky Guacamole / 35
Fresh Tomato Salsa / 36
Garlic Toasts with Tomatoes and Fresh Basil / 37
Garlic Toasts with Cheese, Tomatoes, and Fresh Basil / 37

Breakfast chapter:

Fresh Strawberry-Yogurt Smoothie / 51
Banana-Honey Smoothie / 52

Main Courses chapter:

Old-Fashioned Hamburgers with the Works / 60–61
BBQ Bacon Cheeseburgers / 60–61
Turkey Burgers / 60–61
Pesto Turkey Burgers / 59
Barbecue Tofu Burgers / 62

Pasta and Rice chapter:

Homemade Pesto / 87
The Easiest Couscous / 95
Couscous with Peas and Parmesan / 96

Soups chapter:

Cucumber-Buttermilk Soup / 106
Chilled Gazpacho / 107

Veggies and Salads chapter:

Desserts chapter:

Munchies

Does this sound familiar? Your stomach is threatening to devour itself, you don't have time to cook a meal, and even the fastest delivery place won't get food to your doorstep for at least another half hour. You need something to eat, and you need it now.

Before you start pondering how to turn ketchup into tomato soup, flip through this chapter, where you'll find a variety of easy munchies that can be prepared in 15 minutes or less. Pick one to help you refuel quickly so you can get right back to whatever you were doing before hunger struck.

Or maybe you have a hungry crowd on your hands, and they're threatening to raid your cupboards? These snacks do double duty as party foods that can be made in a flash and are guaranteed to be a hit with your guests.

White Bean-Pesto Dip with Pita Crisps

This super-simple white bean dip is a lot like hummus, and just as addictive. If you're planning to serve the dip to company, go ahead and prepare it a day ahead of time, making sure to keep it safely hidden from your roommate. Serve with some last-minute oven-crisped pita triangles (included in this recipe), plus carrot and celery sticks for the vegetable eaters in the group.

4 pita breads
2 (15-ounce/425 g) cans white beans, drained
3 tablespoons purchased or homemade pesto (page 87)
1/8 teaspoon black pepper

1. Preheat the oven to 425 degrees F (220 degrees C).
2. Cut the pitas in half to make 2 half-circles, and then cut each half into 3 wedges. Spread in a single layer on a baking sheet and bake for 8 to 10 minutes, until crisp and evenly browned.
3. While the pitas bake, place the beans, pesto, and black pepper in a blender. Put the lid on and blend until smooth. Stop the blender every once in a while, remove the lid, and stir the mixture with a spoon.
4. Serve the bean dip with the warm pita crisps.

PREP TIME:
3 minutes

BAKING TIME:
10 minutes

SERVES: *6*

EQUIPMENT:
all-purpose knife, cutting board, baking sheet, can opener, measuring spoons, blender, large spoon or spatula

Garlicky Hummus

This garlicky hummus is so good, it'll make your eyes roll to the back of your head. Serve with regular pita wedges or pita crisps (page 33), or use as a spread for sandwiches.

3 large garlic cloves, peeled
2 (15-ounce/425 g) cans garbanzo beans (chickpeas), drained
1 to 2 lemons
1/2 cup (120 ml) olive oil, plus a few teaspoons to garnish (see Cheap Tip)
1/2 teaspoon salt, or more to taste
1/4 teaspoon black pepper, or more to taste

1. Place the garlic and garbanzo beans in a blender. Cut one of the lemons in half. Holding one of your palms over the blender, squeeze each lemon half over your hand, thereby straining out any seeds.
2. Pour half of the olive oil into the blender, put the lid on, and start blending to chop up the beans. Stop the blender every once in a while to open the lid and stir with a spoon.
3. Add the rest of the olive oil and blend the mixture until it is smooth. If the hummus is thicker than you like, add 2 tablespoons of water.
4. Taste the hummus, then add enough salt and pepper to make it just the way you like it. If it's not tart enough, squeeze in some juice from the remaining lemon.
5. Transfer the hummus to a serving bowl and drizzle a few teaspoons of olive oil on top. Cover and refrigerate any leftovers for up to 2 days.

PREP TIME: *10 to 15 minutes*

SERVES: *6*

EQUIPMENT: *all-purpose knife, cutting board, can opener, blender, liquid measuring cup, large spoon or spatula, measuring spoons, serving bowl*

Cheap Tip

Virgin or extra-virgin? When shopping for olive oil, you'll invariably be faced with this question. Our advice is to go with the virgin olive oil; it's cheaper than the extra-virgin version and has a milder olive flavor. Extra-virgin olive oil is often used to finish a dish, but not so much for everyday cooking.

Chunky Guacamole

Don't you just hate it when a recipe only calls for half of something, like half of a lime? What are you supposed to do with the other half? Well, we've already thought of that: simply use the leftover lime half, cilantro, and jalapeño to make Fresh Tomato Salsa (recipe on page 36).

PREP TIME: *15 minutes*

SERVES: *4 to 6*

EQUIPMENT: *all-purpose knife, cutting board, large spoon, medium bowl, fork, measuring cups and spoons, plastic wrap*

- 3 large ripe (dark and slightly squishy) avocados (see Cheap Tip)
- 1 small red onion, peeled and diced
- 3 tablespoons chopped fresh cilantro
- 2 teaspoons seeded and minced fresh jalapeño
- 1/2 lime
- 1/2 teaspoon salt, or more to taste

1. Start by cutting through an avocado lengthwise, circling the knife around the pit. Twist the avocado halves away from each other so that the avocado splits into two pieces. Pop the pit out with a spoon and throw it away. Repeat this process with the other two avocados.
2. With a large spoon, scoop out the avacado flesh and place in a medium bowl. Mash lightly with a fork. Go easy: You want the finished product to be chunky.
3. Stir in the red onion, cilantro, and jalapeño. Squeeze the lime half over the mixture, picking out any seeds. To get more juice out of the lime, poke the flesh with a fork.
4. Stir in 1/2 teaspoon salt, and then taste to see if you want to add more. Keep in mind that the chips you use for dipping may be salty enough that the guacamole doesn't need to have much added to it.
5. To store the leftover guacamole, place plastic wrap right next to the surface to keep it from turning a nasty-looking brownish color.

Cheap Tip

Avocados bought in bulk are usually cheaper, but they may not be quite as ripe. Buy them several days before you plan to use them, and set them out on the kitchen counter to ripen. You'll know they're finally ripe when they feel slightly squishy; if you press down gently with your finger, the indentation should stay. Store ripe avacados that you're not going to use right away in the refrigerator to make them last longer.

Don't Let This Happen to You

When handling jalapeños—or any hot chile, for that matter—be careful not to touch the seeds and veins inside. They contain a fiery chile oil that will burn whatever it touches, including your skin. Wear rubber gloves to protect yourself, and whatever you do, don't rub your face or eyes. If your skin does start to burn, soap and water won't help; try rubbing with sugar or soaking in milk instead.

Fresh Tomato Salsa

Make sure to pick up a big bag of tortilla chips to use for dipping.

1 pound (450 g) vine-ripened tomatoes (about 2 medium)
1 small onion, peeled and diced
3 tablespoons chopped fresh cilantro
2 teaspoons seeded and minced fresh jalapeño
1 teaspoon olive oil
1/4 teaspoon salt
1/2 lime

1. Using a paring knife, cut the cores out of the tomatoes. Using an all-purpose knife, cut the tomatoes in half crosswise, then squeeze out the seeds into the garbage disposal or a trash can. Dice the tomatoes and transfer to a medium bowl, including the juices.
2. Add the onion, cilantro, jalapeño, olive oil, and salt to the tomatoes; stir to combine.
3. Squeeze the lime half over the mixture, picking out any seeds. To get more juice out of the lime, poke the flesh with a fork.
4. Taste the salsa to see if you want to add more salt. Keep in mind that the chips you use for dipping may be salty enough that the salsa doesn't need to have much added to it. Cover the salsa and store it in the refrigerator until you're ready to serve it.

PREP TIME:
15 minutes

SERVES:
4 to 6

EQUIPMENT:
paring knife, all-purpose knife, cutting board, medium bowl, measuring spoons, large spoon, fork

Garlic Toasts with Tomatoes and Fresh Basil

This has to be the easiest way to make garlic bread: Just toast the bread for a few minutes, and then rub with a raw garlic clove.

PREP TIME:
10 minutes

BAKING TIME:
3 minutes

SERVES: *6*

EQUIPMENT:
baking sheet, liquid measuring cup, all-purpose knife, cutting board, paring knife

6 1/2-inch-thick slices dense, chewy bread (such as country or Italian)
1/4 cup (60 ml) olive oil
2 large garlic cloves, peeled
2 medium ripe tomatoes, cored and thinly sliced crosswise
Salt and black pepper
6 fresh basil leaves, chopped or torn into small pieces

1. Preheat the oven, flipping to the "broil" setting. (A toaster oven set to broil can be used instead.)
2. Place the bread slices on a baking sheet. Measure the olive oil in a liquid measuring cup and drizzle evenly over the bread. Place the baking sheet in the broiler section of the oven and toast for 1 to 3 minutes, or until golden brown. Check on the bread early and often, as it's very easy to burn it in the broiler. Remove from the oven.
3. Rub the tops of the toasts with the peeled garlic cloves. If your toast is crusty and nubby enough, the garlic will be grated by the bread and disappear into it. This is what you want.
4. Divide the sliced tomatoes evenly among the toast slices. Sprinkle lightly with salt and pepper and top with the basil pieces. Serve immediately.

Variation

Garlic Toasts with Cheese, Tomatoes, and Fresh Basil

To turn this snack into a heartier open-faced sandwich, lay a few thin slices of mozzarella or jack cheese underneath the sliced tomatoes.

Sugar & Spice Nuts

These crunchy cinnamon-and-sugar-coated nuts are great for parties (your guests will eat them by the handful), but you don't have to stop there. Try sprinkling them on top of salads or ice cream sundaes.

PREP TIME:
5 to 10 minutes

BAKING TIME:
10 minutes
Makes 2 cups

EQUIPMENT:
2 medium bowls, fork, measuring cups and spoons, spoon, baking sheet

1 egg white
2 cups (200 g) whole walnuts, pecans, and/or almonds (see Cheap Tip)
1/4 cup (50 g) white sugar
2 tablespoons dark or light brown sugar
2 teaspoons ground cinnamon
1/4 teaspoon ground ginger (optional; use if you have it on hand)
Pinch of cayenne
Pinch of salt

1. Preheat the oven to 350 degrees F (180 degrees C).
2. Place the egg white in a medium bowl; beat with a fork until frothy. Add the nuts and toss to coat them with the egg white.
3. In a separate medium bowl, combine the sugar, brown sugar, cinnamon, ginger, cayenne, and salt.
4. Using your hands, lift the nuts out of the egg white and place them in the sugar mixture. Toss with the sugar until evenly coated.

Cheap Tip

When buying nuts, the best and cheapest option is to get the exact amount you need from a store that sells them in its bulk section. Otherwise, buy the smallest package for what you need (the package will say how many cups of nuts are inside). Because nuts have a tendency to go rancid after a few months, store them in the freezer and always taste one for freshness before adding them to a recipe.

5. Transfer the nuts to a baking sheet and spread in a single layer. Bake until the sugar coating is crispy, 10 to 12 minutes. Remove from the oven and transfer to a plate or bowl to cool for at least 10 minutes. The longer the nuts set, the crispier they'll get. Serve warm or at room temperature. Store any leftovers in an airtight bag at room temperature for up to 3 days.

Don't Let This Happen to You

Do you have egg separation anxiety? Consider this recipe a good opportunity to practice your technique; if you do accidentally break the yolk and get some of it mixed up with the egg white, no one will be able to tell the difference. To separate the egg, set up your workspace so that you have two bowls in front of you. One bowl—let's call it Bowl A—will eventually hold the egg white, and another bowl—Bowl B—will hold the egg yolk. Crack the egg on the edge of a bowl or glass and hold it over Bowl A so that only the egg white runs out of the shell into the bowl. Carefully pass the yolk back and forth between the two shell halves until all of the egg white has run out. Now drop the egg yolk into Bowl B. At this point, you can decide what to do with the egg yolk: cover it and refrigerate for up to a day to use in another recipe, or simply throw it away.

Popcorn Flavor Mixes

For a fun, finger-licking twist on microwave popcorn, try one of these Popcorn Flavor Mixes. No microwave? No problem. Just prepare 8 to 10 cups of popped popcorn in an air popper or on the stovetop.

PREP TIME: *2 to 7 minutes*

COOKING TIME: *5 to 7 minutes*

SERVES: *3*

EQUIPMENT: *small microwave-safe bowl or small saucepan, microwave, large bowl, measuring spoons, all-purpose knife, cutting board, spoon, small bowl, large spoon*

4 tablespoons (1/2 stick) butter
1 bag plain microwave popcorn (may be labeled "natural")
Popcorn Flavor Mix (choose one of the following):

- Pizza Popcorn Flavor Mix
  3 tablespoons grated or shredded Parmesan cheese
  1 teaspoon dried oregano
  1 teaspoon minced fresh garlic
  1/4 teaspoon salt
- Garlic Lovers' Popcorn Flavor Mix
  1 tablespoon minced fresh garlic
  1/2 teaspoon salt
  1/8 teaspoon black pepper
- Cinnamon Toast Popcorn Flavor Mix
  3 tablespoons sugar
  1 1/2 teaspoons ground cinnamon

1. Melt the butter in the microwave on the low setting, or in a small saucepan over low heat. Remove from heat.
2. Pop the popcorn in the microwave according to the package instructions (see tip); place in a large bowl.
3. Combine the seasonings for the Popcorn Flavor Mix of your choice in a small bowl.
4. Pour the melted butter evenly over the popcorn and sprinkle with the Popcorn Flavor Mix; toss well to coat.

Don't Let This Happen to You

Popcorn may be easy to make, but it's also very easy to burn. If it does, there's no way to salvage the popcorn, and the smell will haunt your place for days. So don't trust the "Popcorn" button on your microwave. Instead, follow the instructions on the popcorn package to the letter. In most cases, you're supposed to stop microwaving the popcorn when you hear that the pops are 3 seconds or more apart. And be careful when opening the package, or you'll find yourself with a face full of hot steam.

Breakfast

3

When you're racing to get out the door at the beginning of a hectic day, breakfast is the last thing on your mind. Maybe you've overslept or pulled an all-nighter, and you don't have time to cook. That's OK—just don't be tempted to skip breakfast entirely. You've been fasting all night, and if you don't get something in your stomach—even just a slice of toast or cold pizza—your body will kick into starvation mode.

If you need to make breakfast in a hurry, choose a recipe that's especially speedy (look for ones coded with a 15 minutes or less recipe Icon). Best to stick with a smoothie or a quick batch of scrambled eggs to go with your toast. On the weekend, when your mornings are more leisurely, consider pampering yourself with a hot, hearty, comforting breakfast. We can't think of a better way to start the day.

Foolproof Fried Eggs

How do you like to eat a fried egg? Do you break open the yolk and mop it up with your toast? Do you sandwich the egg between two slices of toast and chomp down as the egg yolk drips down your chin? Or maybe you like to spoon out the runny yolk and eat it all by itself? No matter how you choose to enjoy your fried eggs, we'll show you how to make them just the way you like them: over easy, over medium, or sunny-side up.

2 teaspoons butter or vegetable oil
2 large eggs
Pinch of salt
Pinch of black pepper

1. Melt the butter in a small skillet over medium heat until foamy but not brown.
2. Gently crack the eggs into the skillet. The egg whites should start to turn opaque right away; if not, turn up the heat slightly. Sprinkle the eggs with salt and pepper.
3. Cook for 1 1/2 minutes, then loosen each egg with a pancake turner and gently flip over. For eggs over easy, cook on the second side for 30 seconds. For eggs over medium, cook on the second side for 1 1/2 minutes. Use your finger to feel the top of the yolk to see if it's soft or hard enough for you.

COOKING TIME:
5 minutes

SERVES: *1*

EQUIPMENT:
measuring spoons, small skillet, pancake turner

Variation

Eggs Sunny-Side Up

Follow Steps 1 and 2. Cover the eggs and cook without flipping them over until the whites no longer look runny, about 1 1/2 minutes. (The yolks will still be runny.)

Don't Let This Happen to You

If you never have a problem with egg yolks breaking, then maybe you've missed your calling as a short-order cook. For the rest of us, there are two stressful moments when the egg yolks are most likely to break: when the eggs go into the pan, and when the eggs are flipped over. If cracking the eggs directly into the skillet makes you nervous, crack them into a bowl or cup first. That way, you can start over if an egg yolk breaks. If you see any bits of eggshell in there (and it happens to all of us), use one of the eggshell halves to pick it out. Once the eggs are in the skillet and it's time to turn them over, loosen the bottoms with the pancake turner before carefully flipping them over one at a time.

Scrambled Eggs

In about the same amount of time that it takes to make your morning coffee, you can whip up a batch of scrambled eggs. Pop some bread in the toaster, and before you know it, you'll be sitting down to a hot breakfast. To make more servings, simply double or triple the recipe, making sure to use a large skillet.

2 large eggs
1 tablespoon milk or cream
Pinch of salt
Pinch of black pepper
1 teaspoon butter or vegetable oil

1. Crack the eggs into a small bowl. Add the milk, salt, and pepper and beat the mixture with a fork.
2. Melt the butter in a small skillet over medium heat until it turns foamy but not brown.
3. Pour the egg mixture into the skillet. Using a spatula, scrape along the bottom of the skillet to allow the raw egg to run underneath the cooked egg. Cook the eggs until they are no longer runny, about 1 to 2 minutes.

PREP TIME:
3 minutes

COOKING TIME:
2 minutes

SERVES: *1*

EQUIPMENT:
small bowl, measuring spoons, fork, small skillet, spatula or wooden spoon

Don't Let This Happen to You

If your scrambled eggs start to turn brown and crispy, they're trying to tell you that the heat is too high. Keep in mind that the eggs will continue to cook on their own once they're out of the skillet; you'll want to take them off the heat while they're still moist-looking.

Egg-and-Cheese Breakfast Burrito

We fill this breakfast burrito with yummy stuff—scrambled eggs, melted cheese, avocado slices—but don't feel like you need to limit yourself to these ingredients. Warm up leftover beans, rice, or vegetables to include as additional fillings. If you like a lot of heat in your burrito, sprinkle with a few drops of Tabasco sauce before rolling up.

2 large eggs
1 tablespoon milk or cream
Pinch of salt
Pinch of black pepper
1 teaspoon butter or vegetable oil
1 large flour tortilla (burrito-size)
1/4 cup (1 ounce/30 g) shredded cheddar or jack cheese
1 tablespoon fresh or jarred salsa
1/4 ripe avocado, sliced

1. Crack the eggs into a small bowl. Add the milk, salt, and pepper and beat the mixture with a fork.
2. Melt the butter in a small skillet over medium heat until it turns foamy but not brown.
3. Pour the egg mixture into the skillet. Using a spatula or wooden spoon, scrape along the bottom of the skillet to allow the raw egg to run underneath the cooked egg. Cook the eggs until they are just barely runny, about 1 minute. Reduce the heat to low.
4. While the eggs finish cooking, heat a large skillet over medium heat. Place the tortilla in the skillet. Top with the shredded cheese and heat until the cheese starts to melt, about 1 to 2 minutes. (Or, if juggling two skillets is too much for you to handle first thing in the morning, place the tortilla and cheese on a paper towel and microwave on high until the cheese is melted. Don't zap it too long, or the tortilla will be as hard as a Frisbee.)
5. Transfer the tortilla to a plate. Place the scrambled eggs in the center. Top with the salsa. Sprinkle the avocado slices with a pinch of salt and lay on top of the eggs.
6. To roll up the burrito, fold the bottom edge of the tortilla over the filling. Next, fold the right side over the filling. Fold the top edge down, then fold the left side over to completely enclose the filling.

PREP TIME:
7 minutes

COOKING TIME:
5 minutes

SERVES: *1*

EQUIPMENT:
small bowl, measuring cups and spoons, fork, small skillet, spatula or wooden spoon, large skillet or microwave, grater, plate, all-purpose knife, cutting board

Easy Tofu Scramble

This recipe is perfect for that forlorn package of tofu that's staked out a space in the back of your refrigerator. You had such good intentions when you bought it, but . . . it's still there. Here's your opportunity to turn it into something special.

Because tofu has such a mild flavor, it easily serves as a base for many other ingredients. Feel free to add or substitute various kinds of chopped vegetables, such as zucchini, cherry tomatoes, or mushrooms. The more things you include, the better. For extra punch, add a few drops of Tabasco sauce at the last minute.

1 (14-ounce/400 g) container firm or extra-firm water-packed tofu
1 tablespoon vegetable oil
1 medium onion, peeled and chopped
1 small red bell pepper, halved, seeded, and roughly chopped
1 medium garlic clove, peeled and minced
2 cups (100 g) packed baby spinach leaves
1 egg
Salt and black pepper to taste

1. Drain the tofu. Standing over the sink, break the tofu into large chunks. Squeeze the tofu chunks between your hands to press out as much of the excess liquid as you can. Set aside.
2. Heat the oil in a large skillet over medium heat. Add the onion and red bell pepper and cook, stirring occasionally, until the onion is softened, about 4 minutes. Add the garlic and cook for 30 seconds.
3. Add the spinach and reserved tofu to the skillet. Turn the heat up to high. Cook, stirring often, until the tofu is slightly browned. This will take 7 to 12 minutes, depending on the amount of liquid in the skillet. Remove from heat.
4. Crack the egg into a small bowl and beat with a fork. Add the egg to the tofu, stirring to coat evenly. (The heat from the tofu will cook the egg.) Sprinkle with salt and pepper.

Variation

Vegan Tofu Scramble

It's OK to leave the egg out of this recipe, if it's not something you eat. The egg helps to bind the tofu scramble together and give it a bit of color, but it's not essential.

PREP TIME:
10 minutes

COOKING TIME:
12 to 24 minutes

SERVES: *3 to 4*

EQUIPMENT:
measuring spoons, large skillet, all-purpose knife, cutting board, spatula or wooden spoon, small bowl, fork

Weekend-Morning French Toast

The best part of making French toast is deciding what to put on top: a handful of fresh fruit, a drizzle of maple syrup, a dusting of powdered sugar, or all of the above? For extra-fancy French toast, try our Strawberry Topping or Peaches and Cream Topping.

3 large eggs
1/3 cup (75 ml) milk
1/4 teaspoon vanilla extract (optional)
Pinch of salt
1 to 2 tablespoons butter
4 slices bread
Powdered sugar and/or maple syrup

1. Crack the eggs into a small bowl. Add the milk, vanilla, and salt and beat the mixture well with a fork.
2. Melt 1 tablespoon of the butter in a large skillet over medium-high heat until it turns foamy but not brown.
3. Dip a slice of bread into the egg mixture, soaking for at least 5 seconds on each side. White, fluffy bread soaks up the egg mixture quite easily; denser whole-grain bread requires a longer soaking to become saturated.
4. Place the soaked bread in the hot skillet. Repeat the dipping procedure with additional bread slices until the skillet is full. (If you have an extra-large skillet, you may be able to cook all four slices at once.) Flip the slices over once they turn golden on the bottom, about 2 minutes. Cook on the other side for 1 1/2 minutes, or until the bread feels springy, not soggy. Transfer to a plate.
5. If the skillet is dry, add 1 tablespoon butter before cooking the remaining bread slices. Discard any leftover egg mixture.
6. Serve the French toast with powdered sugar, maple syrup, or one of the following toppings.

PREP TIME:
4 minutes

COOKING TIME:
4 to 8 minutes

SERVES: *2*

EQUIPMENT:
small bowl, liquid measuring cup, measuring spoons, fork, large skillet, pancake turner, plate

Strawberry Topping

In a medium bowl, combine 1 pint (225 g) of fresh strawberries and 2 tablespoons of sugar. Mash slightly with a fork so that some of the juice comes out of the strawberries. Let stand at room temperature for 15 minutes, or refrigerate until ready to serve.

Peaches and Cream Topping

In a small bowl, combine 1/2 cup (120 ml) of sour cream, 1 tablespoon of light or dark brown sugar, and 1/4 teaspoon of vanilla extract. Cut a peach into thin slices. Top each slice of French toast with several peach slices and a spoonful or two of the sweetened sour cream.

Fluffy Buttermilk Pancakes

These scrumptious pancakes are thick and puffy with crispy edges. Freeze any leftover pancakes in a freezer bag, and then pop them in the toaster or toaster oven to reheat.

1 cup (140 g) flour
2 tablespoons sugar
1/2 teaspoon baking soda
1/4 teaspoon salt
2 eggs
1 cup (240 ml) buttermilk
1 teaspoon vanilla extract (optional)
2 to 4 tablespoons vegetable oil
2 to 4 teaspoons butter
Butter
Maple syrup or pancake syrup

1. In a medium bowl, mix together the flour, sugar, baking soda, and salt with a fork.
2. In a small bowl, beat the eggs, buttermilk, and vanilla with a fork. Pour into the dry mixture and stir with a fork until mostly smooth.
3. Heat a large skillet over medium heat. Add 1 tablespoon of the oil and 1 teaspoon of the butter. Test the skillet to make sure it's hot enough by putting a drop of batter in the skillet. If it sizzles and starts cooking immediately, the pan is hot enough. If it turns dark brown right away, the pan is too hot.
4. Working in batches, ladle pancake batter into the skillet using a 1/3-cup (80 ml) measure. The batter will spread out to make 4-inch pancakes. Depending on the size of your skillet, you should be able to cook 3 or 4 pancakes at once. Cook until bubbles begin to pop on the tops of the pancakes and the undersides are golden, about 2 minutes. Flip the pancakes over and cook until the other side is golden and the pancakes are cooked all the way through, about 2 minutes. Transfer to a plate.
5. Repeat with the remaining pancake batter, adding 1 tablespoon oil and 1 teaspoon butter to the skillet before each batch. Serve the pancakes with butter and syrup.

PREP TIME:
5 minutes

COOKING TIME:
10 to 14 minutes
Makes 6 (4-inch) pancakes

EQUIPMENT:
medium bowl, measuring cups and spoons, fork, small bowl, liquid measuring cup, large skillet, pancake turner, plate

Variations

Blueberry Pancakes

If you're a blueberry fan, these pancakes will quickly become your favorite. After you pour the pancake batter into the skillet, sprinkle a few fresh or frozen blueberries on top of each pancake. The blueberries may sizzle and pop.

Chocolate Chip Pancakes

Who says you can't have chocolate for breakfast? Add 1/4 cup (30 g) of chocolate chips to the pancake batter just before ladling into the skillet. These rich, gooey pancakes are especially good topped with whipped cream.

Coconut Pancakes

Add 3 tablespoons of sweetened shredded coconut to the pancake batter just before ladling into the skillet. Top the pancakes with sliced bananas and syrup.

Corn Pancakes

Add 1/2 cup (80 g) of frozen corn kernels to the pancake batter just before ladling into the skillet. Top the pancakes with syrup and add some bacon on the side.

Don't Let This Happen to You

You can use margarine in the skillet instead of butter, if that's what you have on hand, but don't use fat-free margarine or spread. It won't melt properly and could waterlog your pancakes.

Skillet-Cooked Bacon

Bacon is simple to make, so long as you remember not to rush it. Keep the heat on medium-low so that the bacon doesn't burn.

COOKING TIME:
10 minutes

SERVES:
2 or more

EQUIPMENT:
large skillet, fork, paper towels

4 or more strips bacon, at least 2 per person

1. Heat a large skillet over medium-low heat. Place the bacon strips flat in the skillet. They should start to sizzle and pop. After about 6 minutes, when the bacon starts to turn brown around the edges, flip the strips over with a fork.
2. Cook on the other side for 2 to 6 minutes, until the strips are as chewy or crispy as you like them to be. Drain on paper towels before serving.

Variation

Microwave Bacon

If you don't have a stove, you can make do by preparing bacon in the microwave. The bacon won't get as brown and crispy as the stovetop version, but hey, it's still bacon.

There's no need to buy a special rack for cooking bacon in the microwave. Just make sure to use a protective layering of paper towels to prevent the bacon from spattering and making a mess.

Layer a plate or paper plate with several layers of paper towels. Place the bacon strips flat on top of the paper towels. Cover them with several more layers of paper towels. Microwave the bacon on the medium-high setting (70 percent) for 2 minutes, and check to see if the bacon is as crispy as you like it. If not, replace the paper towels and heat for another 30 seconds. Keep heating in 30-second increments until the bacon is ready. Depending on the wattage of the microwave, it may take anywhere from 4 to 7 minutes to cook 4 strips of bacon.

Strawberry-Yogurt Smoothie

Breakfast doesn't get any faster or easier than this. Perhaps the best thing about making this smoothie is that you can take it with you as you rush out the door.

1 cup (280 g) frozen strawberries or other berries
1 container (8 ounce/225 ml) vanilla yogurt
1/4 cup (60 ml) milk
1 tablespoon sugar (optional)

Place the strawberries, yogurt, and milk in a blender; blend until smooth, about 1 minute. If it seems that the strawberries are not getting incorporated, stop the blender occasionally and stir with a large spoon or rubber spatula. Taste the smoothie and, if you want, blend in 1 tablespoon sugar to make it sweeter. Pour into a tall glass and drink up.

Variation

Fresh Strawberry-Yogurt Smoothie

Substitute fresh berries for the frozen ones, adding 4 ice cubes to the blender along with the other ingredients.

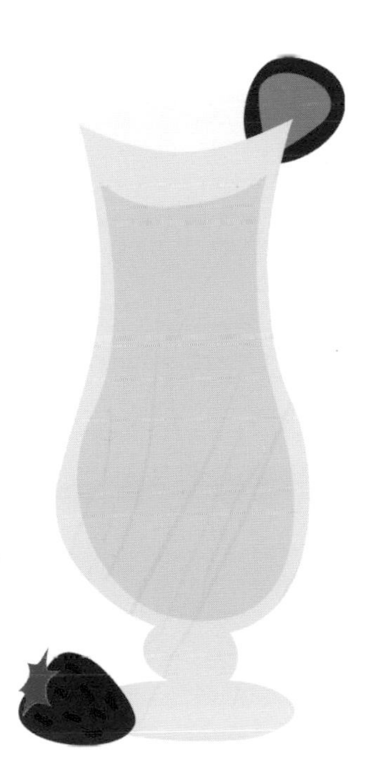

PREP TIME:
3 minutes

SERVES:
1 to 2

EQUIPMENT:
measuring cups and spoons, liquid measuring cup, blender, large spoon or rubber spatula

Don't Let This Happen to You

Nobody likes to wash out a gunked-up blender jar that's been sitting in the sink for ages. To save yourself this nasty chore, do the cleanup right after you pour out the smoothie. Fill the blender jar half full with warm water, put the lid back on, sit it back on the base, and give it a few pulses. The water will wash off the sides of the jar.

Banana-Honey Smoothie

Don't you hate it when bananas turn brown and spotty before you have a chance to eat them? Good news—those ultra-ripe bananas are perfect for making smoothies. The next time you find yourself with more bananas than you can eat, freeze the extras for smoothies. Simply leave the peels on and place the bananas in a freezer bag. When you're ready to make a smoothie, thaw a banana at room temperature for 10 minutes before removing the peel.

PREP TIME:
5 minutes

SERVES: *1 to 2*

EQUIPMENT:
liquid measuring cup, measuring spoons, blender, large spoon or rubber spatula

1 medium banana, peeled
1 container (8 ounce/225 ml) vanilla yogurt
1/4 cup (60 ml) milk
1/4 teaspoon vanilla extract (optional)
4 ice cubes
1 to 2 tablespoons honey

Place the banana, yogurt, milk, vanilla, ice cubes, and 1 tablespoon of the honey in a blender. Blend until smooth, about 1 minute. If it seems like the ingredients are not getting incorporated, stop the blender occasionally and stir with a large spoon or rubber spatula. Taste the smoothie and, if you want it to be sweeter, blend in 1 tablespoon more honey. Pour into a tall glass and drink up.

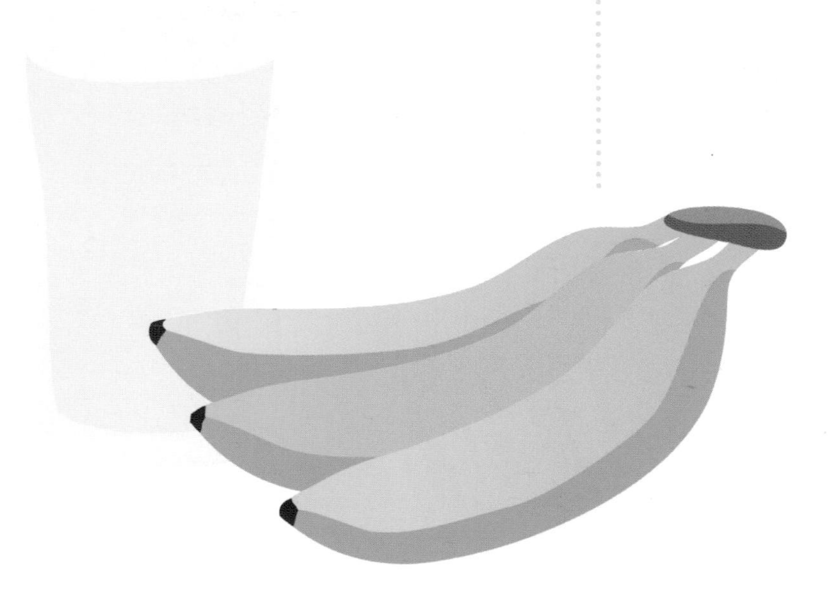

Bagels with Cream Cheese Schmears

A "schmear" is softened cream cheese mixed with other flavors such as fruit, honey, herbs, or smoked salmon. You could buy schmears from a bagel store or supermarket, but it's far cheaper to whip them up yourself.

PREP TIME: *3 minutes*

SERVES: *2*

EQUIPMENT: *measuring cups and spoons, small bowl, fork, knife, toaster*

2 bagels
Choose one of the following schmears:

Fruity Cream Cheese

1/3 cup (3 ounces/85 g) cream cheese
2 tablespoons seedless fruit preserves, such as berry or apricot

Honey and Spice Cream Cheese

1/3 cup (3 ounces/85 g) cream cheese
2 tablespoons honey
1/4 teaspoon ground cinnamon

Chive Cream Cheese

1/3 cup (3 ounces/85 g) cream cheese
1 tablespoon finely minced fresh chives or green onion
Pinch of salt

1. Place the cream cheese in a small bowl; mash with a fork until the cheese is soft and easy to spread. Add the rest of the ingredients for the schmear of your choice. Mash to incorporate into the cream cheese.
2. Slice the bagels in half. Toast, if desired, and spread with the flavored cream cheese.

Don't Let This Happen to You

Bagels can be especially dangerous to cut. If the bagel happens to slip out of your hand while you're cutting it, you could lose control and send the knife flying. To make sure the bagel is secure, hold the top edge with your fingers curled under, keeping them out of the path of the blade. Using a knife with a serrated blade, gently saw back and forth on the bagel, being careful not to exert too much downward pressure. Go slowly, or you may find yourself rushing to the emergency room.

Quick and Easy Cinnamon Crescent Rolls

When you're craving something sweet for breakfast, these luscious, gooey croissants will hit the spot. And because they're made from refrigerated dough, they're almost impossible to screw up. Be warned—once you try these addictive treats, you may never eat frosted pastries out of a box again.

1/4 cup (50 g) sugar
1 teaspoon ground cinnamon
1 (15.5 ounce/440 g) package refrigerated crescent roll dough, such as Pillsbury Grands
4 tablespoons (1/2 stick) butter, softened

Powdered Sugar Glaze

1/2 cup (60 g) powdered sugar
2 teaspoons milk
1/4 teaspoon vanilla extract

1. Preheat the oven to 350 degrees F (180 degrees C). Cover a baking sheet with nonstick aluminum foil.
2. In a small bowl, combine the sugar and cinnamon.
3. Following package directions, open the crescent dough package and unroll the dough. Separate the dough at the precut seams so that you have 6 triangles. Lay the dough triangles flat on the baking sheet.
4. With a knife, spread the butter evenly on top of the dough. Sprinkle with the cinnamon sugar, dividing evenly among the pieces.
5. To roll up each crescent roll, start at the widest edge of the triangle, rolling toward the tip. Bake the rolls until the tops are golden, about 13 to 15 minutes. Remove from the oven and cool on a wire rack.
6. While the rolls are cooling, combine the powdered sugar, milk, and vanilla in a small bowl until smooth. If the glaze seems too thick, add 1/4 teaspoon more milk. Using a spoon, drizzle the glaze evenly over the hot crescent rolls.

PREP TIME:
20 minutes

BAKING TIME:
15 minutes
Makes 6 crescent rolls

EQUIPMENT:
baking sheet, nonstick aluminum foil, 2 small bowls, measuring cups and spoons, spoon, knife, wire rack

Variation

Chocolate-Filled Crescent Rolls

Follow Steps 1 and 3. Sprinkle 1/3 cup (60 g) of chocolate chips evenly on top of the dough triangles before rolling up. Omit the butter, cinnamon sugar, and powdered sugar glaze.

Variation

Cheesy-Garlic Crescent Rolls

Follow Steps 1 and 3. In a small bowl, combine 2 tablespoons of softened butter with 2 cloves of peeled, minced garlic. Spread evenly on top of the dough. Sprinkle 1/3 cup (40 g) shredded cheddar cheese evenly on top of the dough triangles before rolling up. Omit the cinnamon sugar and powdered sugar glaze. Cheesy-Garlic Crescent Rolls aren't just for breakfast—team them with a salad, and you've got lunch.

4 Main Courses

Even if you've never made anything more complicated than PB&J, you'd be surprised at how easy it is to put together a decent meal. We've designed these recipes specifically for beginners, with straightforward, goof-proof instructions. They represent the shortest distance between you and dinner.

The first time you make a recipe, try to stick to it exactly, to get a feel for how the ingredients fit together. After that, feel free to veer off and experiment, adding and subtracting ingredients as you wish. Maybe you like your food to be on the spicy side, or you can't stand the taste of garlic. Follow your taste buds. After all, if you're going to take the time to follow a recipe, the food should turn out just the way you like it.

Let's say you've already tried out Roasted Whole Chicken with Lemon and Herbs (page 80), and the second time around you get the idea to flavor the chicken with oranges instead of lemons. Go for it. If you like the results, jot down a note to remind yourself for the next time. Cooking is about being creative, rather than following a recipe to the letter. As you gain more experience, you'll get a feel for what you can change and what you need to keep the same.

The Ultimate Grilled Cheese Sandwich

Making a grilled cheese sandwich is such a no-brainer that you may not feel the need to consult a recipe. Then again, this twice-as-crispy version of grilled cheese is not like any you've ever had before. Give it a try, and we promise that you'll never make grilled cheese any other way again.

1 tablespoon butter, softened
2 slices white bread
1/2 cup (2 ounces/60 g) shredded cheddar or jack cheese

1. Heat a large skillet over medium heat.
2. Butter both sides of the bread slices. Lay the slices in the skillet and cook until golden, about 1 minute. Flip the slices over.
3. Place the shredded cheese on one of the toasted bread slices. Top the cheesy slice with the other bread slice so that the toasted side faces the cheese. Cook for 30 to 45 seconds, or until golden. Flip the sandwich over. Cook until the cheese is melted, 30 to 45 seconds.

Variation

Fancy Grilled Cheese Sandwich

Mix and match your favorite cheeses, as long as they melt easily. If you feel like splurging on a fancy cheese, try smoked Gouda, fontina, Brie, or Camembert.

PREP TIME:
2 minutes

COOKING TIME:
3 minutes

SERVES: *1*

EQUIPMENT:
large skillet, knife, measuring cups and spoons, pancake turner, grater

Cheese Quesadilla

For a last-minute, super-cheap meal, consider making a quesadilla. Screwing it up is nearly impossible—basically, if the cheese is melted, then the quesadilla is ready. To round out the meal, add a bowl of soup or a green salad.

PREP TIME:
2 minutes

COOKING TIME:
5 minutes

SERVES: *1*

EQUIPMENT:
measuring cups and spoons, large skillet, grater, pancake turner, all-purpose knife, cutting board

1/4 teaspoon vegetable oil
1 large flour tortilla (burrito-size)
1/2 cup (2 ounces/60 g) shredded jack or cheddar cheese

1. Heat the oil in a large skillet over medium heat. Place the tortilla in the skillet. Cover one-half of the tortilla with the shredded cheese. Fold the empty half over the cheesy half.
2. Cook until the underside is toasted, 2 to 3 minutes. Flip over and cook until the other side is toasted, about 1 minute. Slice into wedges and eat while the cheese is still gooey.

Variations

Ham and Cheese Quesadilla

Add a few thin slices of ham to the quesadilla when you add the cheese. Another excellent combination is pastrami and Swiss.

BCT Quesadilla

Crumble 2 slices of cooked bacon and add to the tortilla when you add the cheese. Immediately after you take the quesadilla off the heat, open it up and stick in a few thin tomato slices and a lettuce leaf.

Pesto Turkey Burgers

Mixing ready-made pesto with ground turkey is an effortless way to add a burst of basil-garlic flavor. For an even bigger punch, spread some pesto on the bun instead of mayonnaise. Or mix the mayonnaise with pesto before spreading on the bun. For a Mediterranean twist, try stuffing the turkey burgers inside pita pockets instead of hamburger buns.

1 to 1 1/2 pounds (450 to 680 g) ground turkey
1/4 cup (60 ml) purchased or homemade pesto (page 87) (see Cheap Tip)
1/2 teaspoon salt
Pinch of black pepper
2 teaspoons vegetable oil
4 to 6 hamburger buns
1/4 cup (60 ml) mayonnaise
4 to 6 lettuce leaves
1 medium tomato, sliced
1 small red onion, peeled and thinly sliced

1. Place the ground turkey, pesto, salt, and black pepper in a large bowl, mixing with a fork to incorporate. With your hands, shape the mixture into 1/2-inch-thick patties, 4 to 6 of them, depending on how large you want them to be. (Keep in mind that the burgers will shrink in diameter while they cook.)
2. Heat the vegetable oil in a large skillet over medium heat. Place the burgers in the skillet and cook for 6 to 8 minutes, until the bottoms are golden. Flip them over and cook until no longer pink inside, 6 to 8 minutes.
3. Assemble the burgers by spreading the buns with mayonnaise and topping the turkey burgers with lettuce, tomato, and red onion. Dig in.

PREP TIME:
10 minutes

COOKING TIME:
12 to 16 minutes

SERVES: *4 to 6*

EQUIPMENT:
measuring cups and spoons, large bowl, fork, large skillet, pancake turner, all-purpose knife, cutting board, knife

Cheap Tip

Don't waste your money on jarred pesto, the kind found in the dried pasta section of the supermarket. The fresh stuff, which costs about the same, is sold in round tubs in the refrigerated pasta section. There's a huge difference in flavor between the two.

Old-Fashioned Hamburgers with the Works

Nothing satisfies quite as much as a giant, juicy burger with all the trimmings.

1 to 1 1/2 pounds (450 to 680 g) ground beef
1 large egg
1 medium garlic clove, peeled and minced
1 tablespoon Worcestershire sauce
1/2 teaspoon salt
Pinch of black pepper
4 to 6 cheese slices, such as cheddar or Swiss
4 to 6 hamburger buns
Ketchup
Mustard
4 to 6 lettuce leaves
1 medium tomato, sliced
1 small red onion, peeled and sliced

1. Heat a large skillet over medium heat.
2. Place the ground beef, egg, garlic, Worcestershire sauce, salt, and pepper in a medium bowl, mixing with a fork to incorporate.
3. Using your hands, shape the mixture into 1/4-inch-thick patties, 4 to 6 of them, depending on how large you want them to be. Make a slight indentation in the center of each patty.
4. Turn on the exhaust fan and/or open a window. Place the burgers in the skillet and cook until the bottoms are brown and the sides are no longer red, 4 to 6 minutes. Flip the burgers over and cook for 2 minutes. Lay the cheese slices on top of the burgers. Cook until the cheese is melted and the burgers are no longer pink inside, 2 to 4 minutes.
5. Assemble the burgers with the ketchup, mustard, lettuce, tomato, and red onion. Grab some napkins and dig in.

PREP TIME:
10 minutes

COOKING TIME:
10 minutes

SERVES:
4 to 6

EQUIPMENT:
large skillet, all-purpose knife, cutting board, measuring spoons, medium bowl, fork, pancake turner

Variations

BBQ Bacon Cheeseburgers

Cook 2 strips of bacon per person (see page 50), tearing them in half before placing on the burgers. Top the cheeseburgers with barbecue sauce instead of mustard and ketchup. Omit the lettuce and tomato, but keep the red onion.

Turkey Burgers

Substitute 1 to 1 1/2 pounds (450 to 680 g) ground turkey for the ground beef.

Barbecue Tofu Burgers

Give tofu the burger treatment by dousing it in your favorite barbecue sauce and piling on the toppings.

1 (14 ounce/400 g) package water-packed extra-firm tofu
Salt and black pepper
1 tablespoon vegetable oil
1/4 cup (60 ml) barbecue sauce
4 large hamburger buns
Mayonnaise
4 thin slices red onion
1 large tomato, sliced
4 large lettuce leaves

1. Drain the tofu. With the long edge of the tofu block facing you, cut the tofu into 8 slices, each about 1/2 inch thick. Blot both sides of each slice with paper towels to remove some of the liquid. Sprinkle salt and pepper on both sides.
2. In a large skillet, heat the vegetable oil over high heat. Using a pancake turner, carefully lay the tofu slices in the skillet, watching out for spatters. Cook until the tofu is golden on the bottom, about 5 minutes. Flip over and cook until the other side is golden, about 5 minutes.
3. Turn off the heat. Pour the barbecue sauce over the tofu. Flip the pieces over and nudge them around so that they become evenly coated with the sauce.
4. To assemble each burger, spread a hamburger bun with mayonnaise. Place 2 slices of tofu on the bottom half. Top with 1 slice of red onion and 1 or more slices of tomato. Top with a lettuce leaf and the top half of the bun.

PREP TIME:
7 minutes

COOKING TIME:
11 minutes

SERVES: *4*

EQUIPMENT:
all-purpose knife, cutting board, paper towels, measuring cups and spoons, large skillet, pancake turner, knife

Portobello Mushroom Wraps with Garlic Mayonnaise

Portobellos are huge, meaty mushrooms—perfect for when you want a meatless yet satisfying meal. If you can't find portobello mushrooms, substitute regular button mushrooms, sliced in half. If you don't have tortillas on hand, spoon the mushroom mixture on toast, slap it on a bagel, or stuff it inside a pita.

PREP TIME: *10 minutes*

COOKING TIME: *10 minutes*

SERVES: *2*

EQUIPMENT: *small bowl, measuring spoons, all-purpose knife, cutting board, spoon, large skillet, wooden spoon or spatula*

2 tablespoons mayonnaise
1 medium garlic clove, peeled and minced
Pinch of salt
Pinch of black pepper
2 teaspoons vegetable oil
1 small red onion, peeled, halved lengthwise, and thinly sliced
2 large portobello mushrooms, briefly washed and roughly chopped (see tip on page 64)
Pinch of red pepper flakes
2 flour tortillas

1. In a small bowl, combine the mayonnaise and garlic. Add the salt and pepper. Set aside while you cook the mushrooms.
2. Heat the oil in a large skillet over medium-high heat. Add the onion and mushrooms and cook, stirring often, until soft but not mushy, 7 to 8 minutes. Remove from heat and season with salt, pepper, and red pepper flakes.
3. Divide the mixture between the 2 tortillas. Top with the garlic mayonnaise. To roll up the wrap, fold the bottom edge of the tortilla over the filling. Fold the right side over the filling, then the left side. Leave the top edge open.

(continued on following page)

(continued)

Variations

Portobello Mushroom Wraps with Cheese

Follow Steps 1 and 2. While the mushroom mixture is still in the skillet, add 1/4 cup (1 ounce/30 g) grated cheese and stir to help it melt. Cheddar or jack cheese works well here, or use whatever cheese strikes your fancy. Mozzarella is nice and gooey. Crumbled feta cheese won't melt, but its distinct, salty taste is great with the mushroom flavor.

Portobello Mushroom Wraps with Pesto

Substitute 2 tablespoons of store-bought or homemade pesto (page 87) for the garlic mayonnaise.

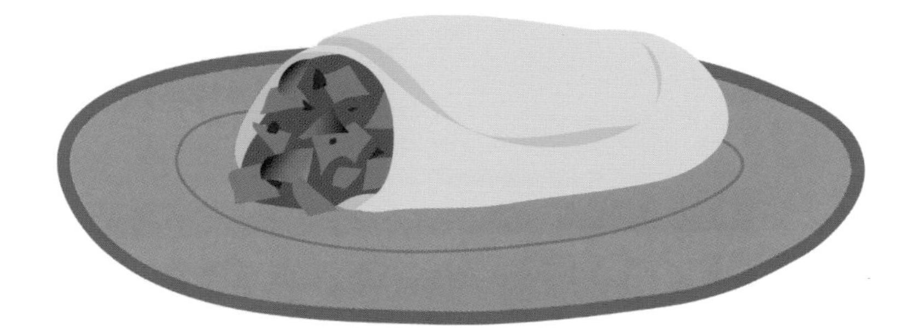

Don't Let This Happen to You

When you clean the mushrooms, don't soak them in water—they will absorb too much liquid and become soggy and worthless. Give the mushrooms a brief rinse under the faucet, using a brush or paper towel to remove any bits of dirt that still cling to the caps.

Indian Potato and Cauliflower Curry

This spicy vegetarian main course has lots of sauce, which makes it the perfect dish to serve over rice or couscous.

1 tablespoon vegetable oil
2 medium onions, peeled and chopped
2 medium russet potatoes, peeled and cut into 1/2-inch chunks
3 medium garlic cloves, peeled and minced
1 small hot chile, such as serrano or jalapeño, seeded and minced (optional)
1 (28 ounce/800 g) can peeled whole tomatoes, with juice
1 small head cauliflower, broken into bite-sized florets, or 1 (12 ounce/340 g) bag cauliflower florets
2 teaspoons curry powder
Salt and black pepper
3 tablespoons chopped fresh cilantro (optional)
1/2 cup (120 ml) plain yogurt (optional)

1. Heat the oil in a large saucepan over medium-high heat. Add the onions and sauté, stirring occasionally, until they become translucent, about 4 minutes.
2. Add the potatoes, garlic, and hot chile, if desired; sauté 1 minute, stirring occasionally.
3. Add the tomatoes, cauliflower, and curry powder. Smash the tomatoes with a large spoon to get out some of the juice. (If it seems there's not enough liquid in the saucepan, don't worry; the curry will get soupier as it cooks.)
4. Bring the mixture to a boil before lowering the heat to medium-low. Cover with a lid and simmer, stirring occasionally, until the potatoes are tender, 25 to 35 minutes.
5. Season with salt and pepper. Stir in cilantro, if desired, and serve with a dollop of yogurt.

PREP TIME:
17 minutes

COOKING TIME:
40 to 50 minutes

SERVES: *4 to 6*

EQUIPMENT:
measuring cups and spoons, large saucepan with lid, all-purpose knife, cutting board, vegetable peeler, large spoon or spatula, can opener

Crispy Fried Chicken Sandwiches

Fried chicken is usually made in a deep-fat fryer—an appliance you most likely don't own and don't really need to have anyway. Another way to give your chicken a crispy coating is to fry it in a skillet in a shallow layer of oil. This is known as pan-frying; you'll find it's much easier and not as messy.

1/4 cup (35 g) flour
1 teaspoon salt
1/2 teaspoon black pepper
1/8 teaspoon cayenne
1/3 cup (80 ml) buttermilk
1/4 cup (60 ml) vegetable oil
2 boneless skinless chicken breasts
2 tablespoons mayonnaise
2 white sandwich rolls, cut in half lengthwise
2 tomato slices
2 lettuce leaves

1. In a small bowl, combine the flour, salt, pepper, and cayenne; transfer the mixture to a plate.
2. Pour the buttermilk into a small bowl.
3. Heat the vegetable oil in a large skillet over medium heat. Dip both sides of each chicken breast in the flour mixture, then the buttermilk, and then the flour mixture again.
4. Transfer the chicken to the skillet and fry until the underside is golden, about 8 minutes. Turn the pieces over and cook until chicken is no longer pink inside, 7 to 9 minutes. The juices should run clear when the chicken is poked with a knife.
5. Line a plate with paper towels; transfer the chicken to the plate to drain.
6. Spread mayonnaise on the rolls, and fill each one with chicken, tomato, and lettuce.

PREP TIME:
5 minutes

COOKING TIME:
20 minutes

SERVES: *2*

EQUIPMENT:
2 small bowls, measuring cups and spoons, spoon, 2 plates, liquid measuring cup, large skillet, tongs or 2 forks, paper towels, knife, all-purpose knife, cutting board

Barbecue Shrimp Pizza

Making homemade pizza is a cinch when you use a prebaked pizza crust. All that's left to do is to mix and match your favorite toppings and then pop it in the oven. This fun pizza combines sweet and smoky flavors; it's like a cross between a Hawaiian pizza and a barbecue chicken pizza, only with shrimp.

1/2 pound (225 g) cooked medium or large shrimp, shells and tails removed (see Cheap Tip)
1 large ready-made pizza crust, such as Boboli
1/3 cup (80 ml) barbecue sauce
1 (8 ounce/225 g) can pineapple chunks packed in juice, drained well
1 cup (4 ounces/115 g) shredded cheese, such as cheddar, jack, and/or mozzarella
1/4 cup (55 g) chopped red onion
3 tablespoons loosely packed fresh cilantro

1. Preheat the oven to 400 degrees F (200 degrees C).
2. Thaw the shrimp, if necessary, by placing in a strainer and running under cold water. Blot with paper towels to dry.
3. Place the pizza crust on a baking sheet. Using the back of a large spoon, spread the barbecue sauce evenly on the pizza crust so that it almost touches the edges.
4. Spread the shrimp evenly on top of the barbecue sauce. Sprinkle with the pineapple chunks and top with the shredded cheese. Sprinkle the red onion on top.
5. Bake the pizza 20 minutes, or until the cheese is melted and bubbly. Remove from the oven. Roughly chop the cilantro and sprinkle on top of the pizza. Slice the pizza into wedges and serve.

Variation

Barbecue Chicken Pizza

Substitute 1/2 pound (225 g) of cooked, chopped chicken for the shrimp.

PREP TIME:
10 minutes

BAKING TIME:
20 minutes

SERVES: *4*

EQUIPMENT:
colander, paper towels, baking sheet, large spoon, measuring cups, can opener, grater, all-purpose knife, cutting board

Cheap Tip

There's big shrimp and there's little shrimp, and as far as prices go, bigger usually means more expensive. Keep your eyes open for bargains, as the price for large shrimp drops by several dollars a pound when it's on sale. The "count" of a shrimp indicates how many of them make up a pound. For this recipe, use either medium (31- to 35-count) or large (21- to 30-count) shrimp, whichever is cheaper.

Skirt Steak Fajitas

Skirt steak is less expensive than other types of steak. And because it comes in thin pieces, it cooks faster, too. We use a dry spice rub to flavor the skirt steak because it's much easier and faster than a marinade.

1/2 teaspoon ground cumin (see Cheap Tip on page 69)
1/2 teaspoon salt
Large pinch of black pepper
Pinch of red pepper flakes
3/4 pound (340 g) skirt steak
1 teaspoon vegetable oil
1 large red onion, peeled, halved lengthwise, and thickly sliced
1 medium red bell pepper, halved, seeded, and cut into strips
1 medium green bell pepper, halved, seeded, and cut into strips
2 medium garlic cloves, peeled and minced
1 lime, cut in half
4 to 8 flour tortillas
Fresh Tomato Salsa, if desired (page 36)
Guacamole, if desired (page 35)

PREP TIME:
10 minutes

COOKING TIME:
15 to 20 minutes

SERVES: *4*

EQUIPMENT:
small bowl, measuring spoons, spoon, large skillet, tongs or fork, plate, all-purpose knife, cutting board

1. In a small bowl, mix the cumin, salt, black pepper, and red pepper flakes. Sprinkle the spice mixture on both sides of the steak.
2. Heat 1/2 teaspoon of the oil in a large skillet over high heat. Turn on the exhaust fan and/or open a window. When the pan is quite hot (but not smoking), add the steak. Brown for 2 minutes, then flip it over. Cook until the steak is only a little pink inside, 2 to 4 minutes (see tip on page 69). Transfer the steak to a plate to rest.
3. If the skillet has burned bits, clean it out or use another one. Add the remaining 1/2 teaspoon oil to the skillet. Add the onion and bell peppers and cook over high heat, stirring occasionally, for 4 to 8 minutes, or until they start to soften and turn brown. They should still be crunchy. Mix in the minced garlic and cook for 30 seconds. Remove from heat.

4. Slice the steak across the grain into 1/4-inch-wide strips. Return the steak and the juices from the plate to the skillet to reheat. Squeeze 1/2 lime over the steak and vegetables. Cut the other 1/2 lime into wedges. Serve the fajitas with tortillas, Fresh Tomato Salsa, Guacamole, and lime wedges.

Don't Let This Happen to You

If your steak turns out tough and chewy, it may be overcooked. To keep the steak tender, use high heat to sear the outside quickly, and check the inside often for pinkness. Keep an eye on the thinner strips of steak, and take them out of the skillet early if they finish cooking before the thicker ones do.

Cheap Tip

When you buy spices such as cumin, look for the smallest container you can find. Better yet, shop at a health food store that sells spices in a bulk section. That way, you can buy the exact amount you want—even as little as 1/2 teaspoon—for much, much less than you would pay for an entire container. Ground spices tend to lose their flavor after six months, so it doesn't pay to stock up.

Sautéed Salmon with Lemon

This crispy seared salmon is a great dish for company; it's beautiful and fancy, yet very simple to make. And while the salmon cooks, you have just enough time to whip up another easy-yet-elegant dish, Asparagus with Browned Butter (page 116).

1 teaspoon butter
2 salmon fillets, about 1 inch thick
1 lemon, cut into 4 wedges
Salt and black pepper

1. Turn on the exhaust fan and/or open a window. Melt the butter in a small skillet over medium-high heat.
2. Place the salmon fillets in the skillet, nicer side down. Sauté until the sides of the salmon are opaque halfway up and the bottoms are golden brown, about 6 minutes.
3. Flip the salmon over and sauté for another 5 to 7 minutes, until it feels fairly firm when you press on it (see tip). (If you're not sure it's cooked all the way through, use a knife to cut it open and peek inside.)
4. Transfer the salmon to a plate, and squeeze a lemon wedge over each fillet.
5. Season with salt and pepper and serve with the 2 remaining lemon wedges.

PREP TIME:
1 minute

COOKING TIME:
12 to 15 minutes

SERVES: *2*

EQUIPMENT:
measuring spoons, small skillet, pancake turner, plate, all-purpose knife, cutting board

Variation

Sautéed Salmon with Citrus

Instead of using lemon, squeeze fresh orange or lime wedges over the salmon.

Don't Let This Happen to You

Fish is notoriously easy to overcook. Before you know it, a fillet that is tender and juicy can turn dry and overcooked. To prevent this from happening, watch the fish carefully to make sure it doesn't cook a minute longer than it has to. As soon as the flesh flakes easily and is opaque all the way through, the fish is done. Another way to tell doneness is to poke the flesh with your finger. If it feels firm rather than springy, then it's high time to take it off the heat.

Sautéed Chicken Breasts

This classic recipe will see you through many a hungry night. Pair it with a vegetable and pasta or couscous, and you have dinner.

1 teaspoon vegetable oil
2 boneless skinless chicken breasts
Salt and black pepper

1. Heat the oil in a large skillet over medium-high heat. Place the chicken breasts, smooth side down, in the hot skillet.
2. Cook until the chicken breasts are browned on the underside, about 8 minutes. Turn the chicken breasts over and cook until they are no longer pink inside, about 8 minutes. Sprinkle with salt and pepper.

COOKING TIME:
18 minutes

SERVES: *2*

EQUIPMENT:
measuring spoons, large skillet, tongs or fork

Variation

Sautéed Chicken Breasts with Lemon and Herbs

Add a squeeze of lemon juice and a sprinkling of chopped fresh herbs such as parsley, thyme, or rosemary to the chicken after it's finished cooking.

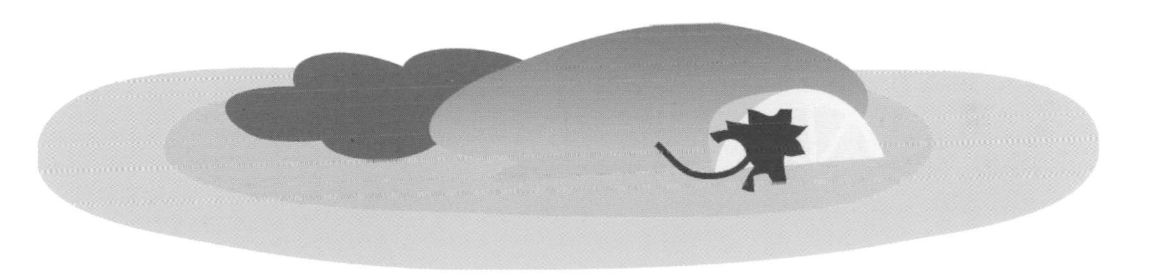

Teriyaki Chicken Breasts

This version takes the basic Sautéed Chicken Breasts recipe on page 71 one step further by adding a salty-sweet sauce. Broccoli is the perfect vegetable to serve along with this dish; the little florets act as sponges and soak up the sauce. Steamed rice (page 92) would round out the meal nicely.

1/4 cup (60 ml) soy sauce
3/4 cup (180 ml) water
3 tablespoons light or dark brown sugar
2 medium garlic cloves, peeled and minced
2 teaspoons peeled and minced fresh ginger (okay to use bottled)
1 1/2 teaspoons cornstarch
1 teaspoon vegetable oil
2 boneless skinless chicken breasts
1 green onion, white and green parts, chopped

1. In a small bowl, mix together the soy sauce, water, brown sugar, garlic, ginger, and cornstarch. Set aside.
2. Heat the oil in a large skillet over medium-high heat. Place the chicken breasts, smooth side down, in the hot skillet.
3. Cook until the chicken breasts are browned on the underside, about 8 minutes. Turn the chicken breasts over and cook until they are no longer pink inside, about 8 minutes. Lower the heat to medium.
4. Pour the reserved soy sauce mixture into the skillet with the chicken and simmer, stirring often, until the sauce thickens (see tip). Turn the chicken breasts over in the sauce a few times, being careful not to splash yourself. Place the chicken breasts on serving plates, top with sauce from the skillet, and sprinkle with the chopped green onion.

PREP TIME:
8 minutes

COOKING TIME:
22 minutes

SERVES: *2*

EQUIPMENT:
small bowl, liquid measuring cup, measuring spoons, all-purpose knife, cutting board, spoon, large skillet, tongs or fork, large spoon

Don't Let This Happen to You

Lumpy sauce is a sign that there was a problem with the cornstarch, the thickening agent. Cornstarch doesn't like to be added directly to hot liquid; it clumps up and makes the sauce lumpy. When adding cornstarch to hot liquid, always dilute it with a small amount of cold liquid first. Once the sauce comes to a boil, the cornstarch will kick in and obediently do its thickening duty.

Variation

Fruity Teriyaki Chicken Breasts

If you have pineapple juice or orange juice on hand, use it in place of the water to add a nice fruity flavor to the teriyaki sauce.

Indian Chicken Curry

You'd think chicken curry would be difficult and time consuming to make. Most of the time it is, especially if you make it the traditional Indian way, which means toasting and grinding your own spices. Since most of us don't have time for that, we've developed a quicker, streamlined version that still captures the bold flavors of Indian food. The cream is optional; if you have it on hand, use it to add richness to the sauce. While the chicken simmers, there's plenty of time to steam some rice to go along with it (page 92).

PREP TIME:
5 minutes

COOKING TIME:
35 minutes

SERVES: *3*

EQUIPMENT:
measuring spoons, large saucepan with lid, all-purpose knife, cutting board, large spoon, can opener

2 tablespoons vegetable oil
1 medium onion, halved, peeled, and sliced
1 tablespoon peeled and minced fresh ginger (OK to use bottled)
2 medium garlic cloves, peeled and minced
1 tablespoon curry powder
1/2 teaspoon salt
Large pinch cayenne (or more to taste)
1 (14 1/2 ounce/410 g) can diced tomatoes, not drained
6 boneless skinless chicken thighs
Pinch of black pepper
2 tablespoons heavy cream or whipping cream (optional)

1. Heat the oil in a large saucepan over medium-high heat. Add the onion and sauté, stirring occasionally, until lightly browned, about 7 minutes.
2. Add the ginger, garlic, curry powder, salt, and cayenne; cook 1 minute. Add the tomatoes and chicken, stirring to coat the chicken with the sauce. Cover the saucepan with a lid.
3. Bring the mixture to a boil, then lower the heat to low and simmer until the chicken juices run clear when pierced with a knife. This should take 20 to 25 minutes.
4. Remove from heat. Stir in the black pepper and cream, if desired. Taste the sauce to see if you want to add more of a kick with the cayenne.

Variation

Chicken Curry Drumsticks

Substitute 6 chicken drumsticks for the boneless chicken thighs. Keep in mind that they will take longer to cook, about 35 minutes.

Crispy Turkey Cutlets

In German cooking, this dish—known as "schnitzel"—is traditionally made with flattened veal or pork tenderloin rather than turkey. You can try it that way, too.

1/3 cup (45 g) flour
1/2 teaspoon salt
1/2 teaspoon black pepper
2 eggs
3/4 cup (84 g) plain or seasoned fine breadcrumbs
1 tablespoon butter
2 to 3 tablespoons vegetable oil
6 turkey cutlets (also called turkey breast fillets)
2 lemons, each cut into 4 wedges

1. Set out three small bowls. Combine the flour, salt, and pepper in the first bowl, beat the eggs with a fork in the second bowl, and place the breadcrumbs in the third bowl.
2. In a large skillet, heat the butter and 2 tablespoons of the vegetable oil over medium-high heat until the butter is melted.
3. To coat a turkey cutlet, dip both sides in the seasoned flour, shaking off the excess. Dip both sides in the egg, then dip both sides in the breadcrumbs, patting the crumbs on with your fingers to help them stick. Place the cutlet in the skillet, and repeat with two more turkey cutlets.
4. Cook for 4 minutes, or until the undersides are golden. Flip over and cook for 4 minutes on the other side. Transfer to a plate and cover with foil to keep warm.
5. Repeat the dipping and frying procedure with the three remaining turkey cutlets, adding 1 tablespoon of oil to the skillet if it seems too dry. Serve the turkey cutlets with lemon wedges.

PREP TIME:
10 minutes

COOKING TIME:
16 minutes

SERVES: *3*

EQUIPMENT:
3 small bowls, measuring cups and spoons, spoon, fork, large skillet, pancake turner, plate, aluminum foil, all-purpose knife, cutting board

Pork Chops with Sautéed Apples and Onions

Pork chop lovers know that these babies are super-simple to prepare: just get out the skillet and fry them on both sides until they're cooked all the way through. Cooking doesn't get much easier than this.

2 teaspoons butter
2 teaspoons vegetable oil
1 small onion, peeled and chopped
1 tart apple, such as Granny Smith, peeled or unpeeled
Pinch of salt
Pinch of black pepper
Pinch of sugar
Pinch of ground cinnamon (optional)
2 teaspoons chopped fresh parsley
2 pork chops (boneless or bone-in)

PREP TIME: *5 minutes*

COOKING TIME: *30 minutes*

SERVES: *2*

EQUIPMENT: *large skillet, measuring spoons, all-purpose knife, cutting board, wooden spoon or spatula, fork, medium bowl*

1. In a large skillet, heat the butter and 1 teaspoon of the vegetable oil over medium-high heat until the butter melts. Add the chopped onion and sauté, stirring occasionally, until it starts to turn golden, about 5 minutes.
2. While the onion cooks, cut the apple into quarters. Cut out the cores, then cut each apple quarter into 4 or more slices.
3. Add the apple slices to the skillet. Add a pinch each of salt, pepper, and sugar. Sauté, stirring occasionally, until the apples are tender when pierced with a fork, about 5 minutes. Transfer the apples and onions to a bowl. Stir in the cinnamon and parsley.
4. In the same skillet, heat the remaining 1 teaspoon oil over medium-high heat. Place the pork chops in the skillet. Sprinkle the tops with salt and pepper, then flip the pork chops over. Sprinkle salt and pepper on the other side.
5. Cook the pork chops for 4 minutes, or until golden brown. Flip them over and cook until they are no longer pink inside, about 4 to 8 minutes, depending on how thick the pork chops are.
6. Warm the apples and onions in the skillet by placing them on top of and around the pork chops.

Basic Steak

Why would you bother cooking a steak at home when you could just order one at a restaurant? For one thing, cooking your own steak is incredibly easy and a heck of a lot cheaper than going to a steakhouse. Even a mediocre cut of beef at a restaurant is more expensive than a primo slab of meat that you buy and cook yourself.

What kind of steak should you buy? Well, if money is no object (or someone else is footing the bill), and you like a lean and tender cut, filet mignon is the steak to go for. Use a small amount of vegetable oil in the skillet to keep the steak from sticking.

T-bone and porterhouse steaks are delicious bone-in cuts, but again, they can be pricey. They have a little more fat and are quite tasty. Rib-eye steak is a bit chewy and full of flavor; we think it's always a good choice. Another one of our favorites is skirt steak, a perfect cut for fajitas (see page 68). Skirt steak has a rich, delicious flavor that goes well with marinades and spice rubs. Last but not least, sirloin steaks are tasty and relatively easy on the wallet.

In the following basic recipe, you'll use a cooking technique called pan-broiling, which means cooking in a skillet over high heat using little or no oil. Notice that there are no exact cooking times listed because they vary so much from steak to steak; only you will be able to tell how rare or well done you like the steak to be.

1 steak of your choice, 1 to 2 inches thick (see Cheap Tip on page 77)
1/4 teaspoon vegetable oil (only if you're cooking a very lean steak like filet mignon)
Pinch of salt
Pinch of black pepper
Steak sauce (optional)

1. Turn on the exhaust fan and/or open a window. (When done right, pan-broiling can be a smoky endeavor.)
2. Make sure the steak is dry, patting it with paper towels if necessary.
3. Heat a large skillet over high heat. (If you like your steak well done, use medium-high heat.) Add the vegetable oil if you're cooking a steak that has very little fat.

PREP TIME:
5 minutes

COOKING TIME:
5 to 15 minutes

SERVES: *1*

EQUIPMENT:
paper towels, large skillet, measuring spoon, tongs or two forks, steak knife

4. Once the skillet is very hot, add the steak. Cook the steak on both sides until it is done to your liking. To check for doneness, cut it open a little; if it's too pink inside, cook it a little longer and check again.
5. Remove the steak from heat and season with salt and pepper. Serve with steak sauce, if desired.

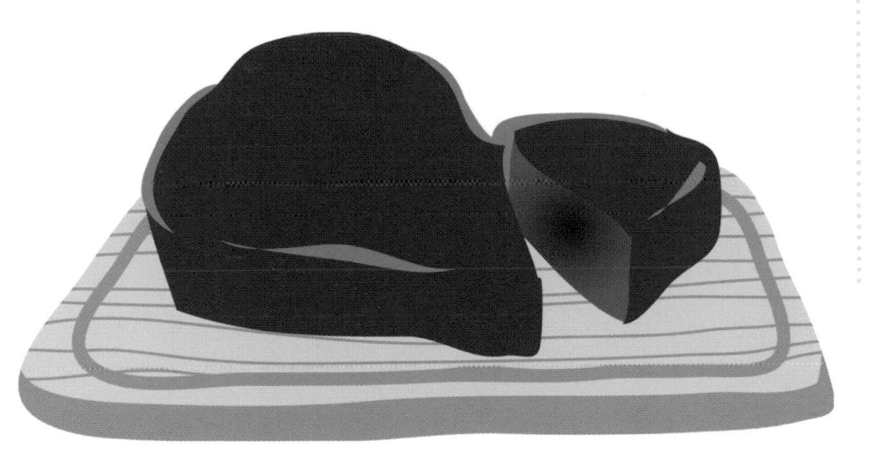

Cheap Tip

No matter which kind of steak you choose, always look for ones that are on sale. Often you can buy steaks in larger packs at a reduced price. If you do buy extra steaks to freeze, make sure you store them in plastic bags designed especially for the freezer.

Pot Roast with Onions, Potatoes, and Carrots

Don't be put off by the length of this recipe: Pot roast is very low maintenance and a cinch to make. After you brown the outside of the meat on the stovetop, you stick the roast in the oven and basically forget about it for several hours.

Leftover pot roast is even better the next day. To store the leftovers, place them in a covered container in the refrigerator. Skim the fat off the top of the liquid before reheating.

1 tablespoon vegetable oil
1/2 to 1 teaspoon salt
2 to 3 pounds (1 to 1.5 kg) boneless beef chuck roast, preferably center cut (see Cheap Tip on page 79)
1 large onion, peeled and roughly chopped
3 medium garlic cloves, peeled and minced
1 to 2 medium potatoes
2 to 4 medium carrots
2 cups (460 ml) or more store-bought beef broth
3 or 4 whole sprigs of fresh thyme (optional, but nice)
Salt and black pepper to taste
A few dashes of Worcestershire sauce (optional)

1. Preheat the oven to 350 degrees F (180 degrees C).

2. Check to see if your baking dish is safe to use on the stovetop. If not, use a large skillet for the browning step instead. Place the baking dish or skillet on the stove over high heat. Turn on the exhaust fan and/or open a window. Add the vegetable oil and heat for 3 to 4 minutes.

3. Sprinkle salt on all sides of the pot roast. Place the roast in the baking dish or skillet and brown the surface for 10 minutes, flipping it over occasionally so that all sides get brown.

4. While the meat browns, prepare the vegetables. Estimate the amount of extra room that you will have in the baking dish, and use the larger or smaller amount of potatoes and carrots accordingly. Peel the potatoes and cut into 1-inch chunks. Scrub the carrots and cut into 1-inch chunks. Set the potatoes and carrots aside in a large bowl filled with cold water. The water will keep the potatoes from turning brown.

PREP TIME:
20 minutes

COOKING TIME:
3 hours

SERVES: *4 to 6*

EQUIPMENT:
large ovenproof dish with lid, measuring spoons, fork or tongs, all-purpose knife, cutting board, large bowl, liquid measuring cup, plate

5. If you used a skillet to brown the meat, transfer the pot roast to the baking dish. Add 1/4 cup (55 ml) of beef broth to the skillet, using a fork to scrape up any browned bits. Add this liquid to the baking dish as well.
6. Sprinkle the onion and garlic pieces around the pot roast. Add the thyme, if desired. Add enough beef broth to the baking dish so that the liquid comes halfway up the sides of the pot roast; the amount of broth you use will depend on the size and shape of the dish.
7. Cover the baking dish with the lid. Place in the oven and bake for 2 1/2 hours.
8. Drain the potatoes and carrots. Add them to the baking dish, pushing them down so that the broth covers them. Cover with the lid and bake 15 minutes. Uncover and bake another 15 minutes, or until the meat and vegetables are very tender.
9. Take the dish out of the oven and transfer the pot roast and vegetables to a plate. Taste the liquid (be careful, it's hot) and add salt and pepper to taste. Add Worcestershire sauce, if desired.
10. Cut the pot roast into pieces. Serve with the vegetables and top with some of the pan sauce.

Cheap Tip

Pot roast is much cheaper than other cuts of beef because it's tough and needs to cook for a long time in order to become tender. To pick out a pot roast, go to the supermarket meat department and look for a section labeled "Roast/Braise." The selection you'll find there will include cuts like rump roast, chuck roast, and brisket. We recommend using a center-cut roast because it has more marbling and therefore will be very tender. Brisket would work well, too. Roasts come in various shapes and sizes; make sure to choose one that's small enough to fit inside your baking dish.

Roasted Whole Chicken with Lemon and Herbs

This is the perfect dish to make when you want to impress a dinner guest. There's something about a roasted chicken that inspires a lot of "oohs" and "ahs" when it arrives at the dinner table. What you don't need to mention to your guest is that the chicken is ridiculously easy to make: Just rub the skin with butter and garlic, stuff some herbs and lemon in the cavity, and pop in the oven for about an hour.

You can make a good roasted chicken without using fresh herbs. The chicken will still be quite tasty, just not as fragrant. The lemon, however, is a must.

1 3- to 4-pound (1.4 to 1.8 kg) whole chicken (see Cheap Tip on page 81)
2 tablespoons butter, softened
2 medium garlic cloves, peeled and minced
Salt and black pepper
1 lemon, cut in half
Large handful of fresh rosemary and/or thyme sprigs (optional)

1. Preheat the oven to 400 degrees F (200 degrees C).
2. Remove the giblets and neck from the chicken cavity. Throw away, or reserve to bake with the chicken. Rinse chicken with cold water. Blot the chicken skin well with paper towels to remove excess moisture.
3. Using your hands, massage the butter all over the outside of the chicken (see tip). Rub the minced garlic over the chicken. Sprinkle the skin with salt and pepper.
4. Place the lemon halves and half of the fresh herbs inside the chicken cavity. Lay the rest of the herbs in the baking dish. Set the chicken on top of the herbs, breast side up. Add the giblets and neck to the dish, if desired.
5. Place the chicken in the oven and roast for 40 minutes.
6. Using 2 wooden spoons or tongs, hold the chicken at both ends and carefully turn it over so that the breast faces down. (Be careful not to get spattered by the hot butter in the bottom of the baking dish.) Roasting the chicken upside down like this will ensure that the breast meat stays moist.

PREP TIME:
10 minutes

BAKING TIME:
1 hour

SERVES: *4 to 6*

EQUIPMENT:
paper towels, all-purpose knife, cutting board, large ovenproof dish, 2 wooden spoons or tongs

7. Roast for 10 minutes, then check to see if the chicken is cooked all the way through. When you pierce one of the thighs with a knife, the juices should run clear with no traces of pink. If not, roast for an additional 10 to 15 minutes, or until the chicken is done. Remove from the oven.
8. Turn the chicken back over so that the breast faces up. Let it rest for 5 minutes; this allows the juices to redistribute through the bird. Serve the chicken along with some of the melted herb butter from the baking dish. Set out plenty of napkins.

Don't Let This Happen to You

When you massage butter into the chicken skin, you may find that the butter sticks to your fingers instead of the chicken. To prevent this, dry the chicken well with paper towels before rubbing it with the butter.

Cheap Tip

There's no need to feel intimidated about buying a whole chicken. They cost less per pound than precut chicken pieces do, and they're just as easy to cook. Plus, you'll end up with leftovers that you can use in sandwiches and salads for the next 2 or 3 days. When whole chickens go on sale, it's a good idea to buy one or two to store in the freezer. Start thawing the chicken in the refrigerator 2 days before you want to use it.

Roasted Turkey Breast with Cranberry-Orange Sauce

If you've invited a handful of people over for holiday dinner, there's no need to wrestle with a huge turkey. Go easy on yourself, and roast a turkey breast instead. It's much smaller and easier to handle. Plus, the breast meat stays juicy because you don't have to cook it to death while the rest of the bird finishes roasting.

Leftover turkey breast is great to have around for making sandwiches. Just slice up the roast turkey, whack it on some bread with a bit of mayo, and call it lunch.

1 turkey breast half, 3 to 4 pounds (1.4 to 1.8 kg)
1 teaspoon vegetable oil
Salt and black pepper
Cranberry-Orange Sauce (recipe follows)

1. Preheat the oven to 350 degrees F (180 degrees C). Line a large ovenproof dish with aluminum foil.
2. Place the turkey breast in the dish, skin side up. Using your fingers, rub oil all over the turkey skin. Sprinkle with salt and pepper.
3. Place the turkey in the oven and roast until the meat releases clear juices when pierced with a knife, 15 to 20 minutes per pound of turkey (45 to 80 minutes total, depending on the size of the turkey breast).
4. Let the turkey rest for 10 minutes to allow the juices to redistribute. Cut into thin slices and serve with cranberry-orange sauce.

PREP TIME:
2 minutes

BAKING TIME:
45 minutes to 1 1/4 hours

SERVES: *4 to 6*

EQUIPMENT:
large ovenproof dish, aluminum foil, measuring spoons, knife

Cranberry-Orange Sauce

There's nothing wrong with serving jellied cranberry sauce from a can, but if you have the time, making your own cranberry sauce from scratch is surprisingly quick and easy. With a little foresight, you can make it up to 3 days ahead and have it waiting in the refrigerator.

1 (12 ounce/340 g) package fresh cranberries (see Cheap Tip)
1 cup (200 g) sugar
1 medium orange, or 1/4 cup (60 ml) orange juice

1. Place the cranberries and sugar in a medium saucepan.
2. Slice the orange in half and squeeze the juice into a liquid measuring cup. Use a spoon to pick out the seeds. If necessary, add water to the juice to make 1/4 cup (60 ml) liquid. Add to the cranberry mixture.
3. Place the saucepan over high heat. Bring to a boil, then reduce the heat to low so that the cranberry mixture is just bubbling. (Don't stand too close to the stove or you might stain your clothes.) Simmer, stirring occasionally, until the cranberry skins pop and the foam subsides, about 5 minutes. Remove from heat.
4. Transfer the cranberry sauce to a serving bowl. Let it cool down, and then refrigerate until ready to serve (it will thicken as it cools). If you rinse the sticky saucepan right away with hot water, the cleanup will be much easier.

PREP TIME:
4 minutes

COOKING TIME:
10 minutes

SERVES: *4 to 6*

EQUIPMENT:
measuring cups, medium saucepan, all-purpose knife, cutting board, liquid measuring cup, spoon, large spoon

Cheap Tip

It makes sense to stock up on fresh cranberries when they're in season, usually from October to December. Not only are they on sale at that time; they're usually not available the rest of the year. Stick the cranberries in the freezer, right in the bag they came in, and freeze for up to a year. That way you'll always have some on hand to make cranberry sauce.

5 Pasta and Rice

If you think of yourself as someone who has no business being in the kitchen, then pasta and rice may be right up your alley. If you can boil water, you can make either one. And if you can't boil water—no worries—make couscous (pronounced KOOS-koos), an easy, no-cook side dish that takes only minutes to prepare.

Because pasta and rice are such versatile staples, it's good to have them lurking in your cupboard for those times when you have no idea what to make for dinner. To keep you out of the pasta-topped-with-jarred-sauce rut, we offer a variety of easy recipes, including some trusty favorites and a few options that will encourage you to branch out. So put a pot of water on to boil, and let's get started.

Basic Pasta

Cooking pasta is so easy that you don't really need to consult a recipe. Here are the basics to help you make sure your pasta comes out right and not in a mushy, tangled mess.

4 quarts (4 liters) water
Large pinch of salt
1 (16 ounce/450 g) package pasta (any kind) (see Cheap Tip)

1. Fill a large saucepan with at least 4 quarts (4 liters) of water (see tip). (If you only want to make half a package of pasta or so, use half as much water.) Add a large pinch of salt. Bring to a boil over high heat.
2. Add the pasta to the saucepan and stir to make sure all of the pieces separate. To keep the pasta from boiling over, turn the heat low enough so that the water is still boiling but not foaming up. Stir every 2 minutes or so to prevent clumping.
3. Taste the pasta 2 minutes before the package directions say it will be done. If it's tender enough for your liking, drain it in a colander, shaking the pasta a bit to get out most of the water. If it's not tender enough, boil 1 more minute before tasting again. Don't rinse the pasta unless you plan to use it in a salad; the starch clinging to the pasta will help the sauce to stick.

Don't Let This Happen to You

If your pasta clumps, it's a sign that you need to use more water. Four quarts of water may seem a bit extreme, but pasta needs a lot of water to swim around in. The less room it has in the saucepan, the more likely it is to clump together.

COOKING TIME: *varies, depending on the pasta*

SERVES: *6 to 8*

EQUIPMENT: *largest saucepan you have, liquid measuring cup, large spoon, colander*

Cheap Tip

Fresh pasta is considerably more expensive than dried pasta but can be nice to serve on a special occasion. You can buy dried pasta from the bulk section, getting only as much as you need, but there won't be any package instructions to tell you how long to cook it. (Check a packaged version of the pasta at the store and make a note to remind yourself.)

Pasta Sauce with Turkey Meatballs

Maybe you think you don't have enough time to make pasta sauce from scratch. We suspect you do—consider all that time you spend waiting for the water to come to a boil, and then the time you spend waiting for the pasta to finish cooking. If you're coordinated enough to juggle two saucepans at once, then you can make a tasty homemade pasta sauce that's guaranteed to knock the socks off anything that comes out of a jar.

Start boiling the water for pasta before you prepare the sauce. Once the meatballs are happily cooking in the sauce (Step 6), boil the pasta. That way, both pasta and sauce will be ready at the same time. For extra flavor, add a handful of chopped fresh basil or a spoonful of pesto to the sauce at the last minute.

Pasta Sauce

1 teaspoon vegetable oil
1 medium onion, peeled and chopped
2 medium garlic cloves, peeled and minced
1 (28-ounce/800 g) can crushed tomatoes

Turkey Meatballs

1/2 pound (8 ounces/250 g) ground turkey
1 medium garlic clove, peeled and minced
2 tablespoons grated or shredded Parmesan cheese
1/4 teaspoon salt
Large pinch of black pepper

1. Heat the oil in a medium saucepan over medium-high heat. Add the onion and sauté, stirring occasionally, until it turns translucent, about 5 minutes.
2. Add the garlic and tomatoes. Bring the sauce to a simmer, then turn the heat to low.
3. Cover the saucepan with the lid and simmer, stirring occasionally, for 10 minutes. Meanwhile, get to making the meatballs.
4. In a medium bowl, mix together the ground turkey, garlic, Parmesan cheese, salt, and pepper, using a fork to combine. With your hands, roll the mixture into 8 to 10 walnut-sized meatballs.
5. Carefully drop the meatballs into the sauce. Do not stir the sauce once the meatballs have been added.
6. Cover the saucepan and simmer until the meatballs are cooked all the way through, about 15 minutes. Taste the sauce and add salt and pepper to your liking. Serve over spaghetti or your favorite pasta.

PREP TIME:
10 minutes

COOKING TIME:
40 minutes

SERVES:
2 to 3

EQUIPMENT:
measuring spoons, medium saucepan with lid, all-purpose knife, cutting board, wooden spoon or heatproof spatula, can opener, medium bowl, fork

Variation

Meatball Sandwich

Heat up the leftover meatballs and pasta sauce and stick inside a French roll. Top with shredded mozzarella cheese.

Homemade Pesto

Nothing—and we mean nothing—can compare to the intense basil flavor of freshly made pesto. This is another example of a sauce that you have plenty of time to pull together while you're cooking the pasta—just get out the blender and whirl away.

Pesto isn't just for pasta. It's good to have on hand in the fridge or freezer for whenever a dish needs a flavor boost. Stir into soups (including ramen noodles), dollop on potatoes, chicken, or fish, or mix with cream cheese to make a spread for bagels and crackers.

1/4 cup (25 g) unsalted nuts of your choice (except peanuts) (see Cheap Tip)
3 medium garlic cloves
1/4 to 1/2 cup (60 to 120 ml) olive oil
1/3 cup (35 g) grated or shredded Parmesan cheese
2 cups (50 g) packed fresh basil leaves
Pinch of salt
Pinch of black pepper

1. Chop the nuts and place them in a blender. Peel the garlic, cut into a few pieces, and place in the blender.
2. Add 1/4 cup of the olive oil to the blender. Put the lid on and blend the mixture until it is fairly smooth.
3. Add the Parmesan cheese and basil and blend until they are incorporated into the sauce. You may need to stop the blender every once in a while to stir the mixture with a large spoon or rubber spatula. Add more oil if the sauce looks too dry; it should be thick and liquid, but without pools of oil gathering when the blender stops. Season with salt and pepper to taste.
4. Follow the instructions for cooking pasta on page 85. Before you drain the pasta, save 1/2 cup of the cooking water.
5. Transfer the drained pasta to a large bowl, add the pesto, and toss to coat. Add a little of the reserved cooking water if the mixture seems too dry and does not coat the pasta easily. If you have leftover pesto, freeze it in a freezer bag.

PREP TIME:
12 minutes
Makes 3/4 cup (180 ml), enough to coat 1 pound (450 g) of cooked pasta

EQUIPMENT:
measuring cups, all-purpose knife, cutting board, blender, liquid measuring cup, large spoon or rubber spatula, large bowl

Cheap Tip

Usually pesto is made with pine nuts, but they can be relatively expensive. Walnuts and almonds, which are a bit cheaper, also make excellent pesto, and their skins add nice brown flecks to the bright green sauce.

Fresh basil is plentiful and inexpensive in the summertime. Look for a store that sells it cheaply in large quantities.

Fettuccine Alfredo

Fettuccine Alfredo is the perfect pasta to serve to company because it seems complicated to make, but in reality, it takes very little effort. Once the pasta finishes cooking, you only need a minute to make the rich, creamy sauce that goes with it. Round out the meal with a fresh loaf of crusty bread—easy to find in almost any grocery store—and a Basic Green Salad (page 117).

Large pinch of salt
8 ounces (225 g) fettuccine
2 tablespoons butter
1/2 cup (110 ml) heavy cream or whipping cream
1/2 cup (50 g) grated Parmesan cheese
Pinch of salt
Large pinch of black pepper

1. Fill a large saucepan with at least 2 quarts (2 liters) of water. Add a large pinch of salt. Bring to a boil over high heat.
2. Add the fettuccine and cook according to package directions, stirring occasionally. (For pointers on cooking pasta, see page 85.) Drain the pasta.
3. In the same saucepan that you used to cook the pasta, melt the butter over medium-low heat. Return the pasta to the saucepan.
4. Add the cream and Parmesan cheese, stirring to coat the pasta evenly with the sauce. Heat until warmed through, about 1 minute (see tip). Add a pinch of salt and a large pinch of pepper, and serve immediately.

COOKING TIME:
25 to 35 minutes

SERVES: *2*

EQUIPMENT:
large saucepan, large spoon, colander, liquid measuring cup, measuring cups and spoons

Don't Let This Happen to You

Be careful not to let the cream sauce cook for longer than a minute. The cream will thicken too much and the cheese will clump up, making the sauce too thick to coat the pasta.

Asian Noodles with Spicy Peanut Sauce

If you like Thai peanut dipping sauce, you'll love this hot and spicy noodle dish.

1 (12 ounce/340 g) package udon or soba noodles (see Cheap Tip on page 90)
1/2 cup (130 g) creamy (not chunky) peanut butter
1 medium garlic clove, peeled and minced
2 tablespoons soy sauce
1/4 teaspoon sugar
1/4 teaspoon cayenne, or more to taste (see tip, page 90)
1 to 2 limes
1/2 cup (120 ml) hot water
1 small carrot, peeled and shredded
2 green onions, white and green parts, chopped

1. Fill a large saucepan with at least 3 quarts (3 liters) of water. Bring to a boil over high heat.
2. Add the noodles to the boiling water and cook, stirring occasionally, until they are tender, 8 to 10 minutes.
3. While the noodles cook, place the peanut butter, garlic, soy sauce, sugar, and cayenne in a large bowl.
4. Cut a lime in half. Squeeze the juice from both lime halves into the bowl, picking out any seeds. To get more juice out of the lime, poke the flesh with a fork.
5. Add 1/2 cup hot water to the bowl. Using a fork, stir to combine. Taste the sauce to see if you want to add more cayenne or lime juice.
6. Drain the noodles and transfer to the bowl. Add the carrot and green onion and toss to combine.

PREP TIME:
10 minutes

COOKING TIME:
20 to 30 minutes

SERVES: *4*

EQUIPMENT:
large saucepan, large spoon, measuring cups and spoons, all-purpose knife, cutting board, large bowl, fork, liquid measuring cup, colander, vegetable peeler, grater

(continued on following page)

(continued)

Variation

Vegetables with Spicy Peanut Sauce

Make the peanut sauce by itself (Steps 3 to 5), and use as a dip for fresh vegetables like carrots, celery, jicama, and red bell pepper.

Cheap Tip

Look for soba or udon noodles in the Asian section of the supermarket (not the pasta section). If you live near an Asian grocery store, buy the noodles there instead; you'll find much more variety and a cheaper price. Health-food stores are also a good bet. In a pinch, you can substitute spaghetti or linguine.

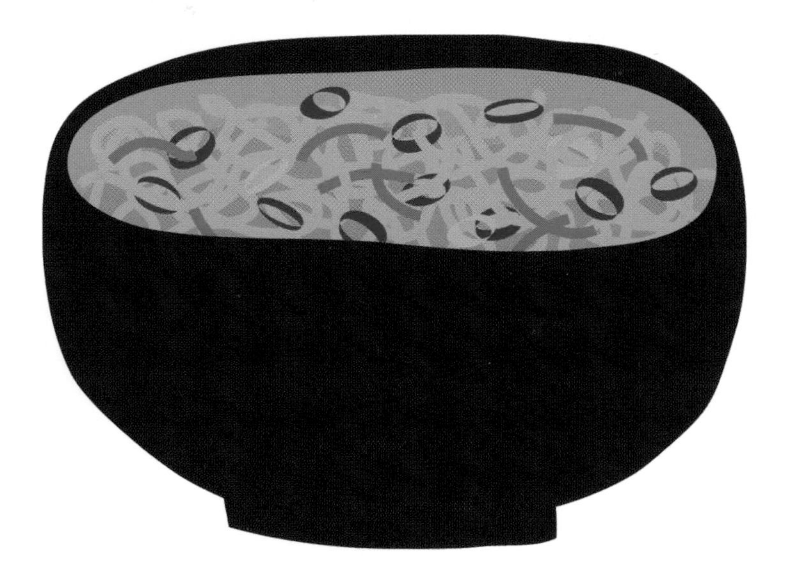

Don't Let This Happen to You

If a dish turns out to be too spicy, there's usually not much you can do to rescue it. Our strategy for avoiding this problem is to start with a small amount of spice and then add more according to your taste. If you have a particularly low tolerance for spicy food, make this recipe with only half the amount of cayenne—you can always add more later on if you want.

Pan-Fried Asian Dumplings with Dipping Sauce

Asian dumplings—also known as potstickers or gyoza—are surprisingly quick and easy to prepare. Pan-frying gives them a browned, crispy bottom.

2 tablespoons soy sauce
2 tablespoons rice vinegar
Pinch of sugar
2 to 3 teaspoons vegetable oil
8 to 10 frozen meat or vegetable Asian dumplings (no need to thaw)

1. To make the dipping sauce, combine the soy sauce, rice vinegar, and sugar in a small bowl. Set aside.
2. Heat a large skillet over medium-high heat. Add enough oil to the skillet to thinly coat the bottom.
3. Add the dumplings to the skillet. Cook without flipping until the undersides start to turn golden brown and the wrappers start to turn translucent, about 6 minutes. The time may vary, depending on how frozen the dumplings are.
4. Add 2 tablespoons of water to the skillet. (Don't stand too close; you want to be careful not to get spattered by the oil.)
5. Cover with the lid, reduce the heat to medium-low, and steam until the skins become mostly translucent, about 2 minutes. Serve immediately with the dipping sauce.

PREP TIME:
2 minutes

COOKING TIME:
12 minutes

SERVES: *1*

EQUIPMENT:
measuring spoons, small bowl, spoon, large skillet with lid, tongs or fork

Basic Rice

This recipe calls for long-grain rice, which is a good basic rice for everyday cooking. You can also try different kinds of aromatic rice, such as jasmine or basmati.

2 cups (475 ml) water
Pinch of salt
1 cup (180 g) long-grain white rice (see Cheap Tip)

1. Place 2 cups of water in a medium saucepan. Add a pinch of salt. Bring to a boil over high heat.
2. Add the rice, cover with the lid and turn the heat to low (see tip).
3. Simmer until the rice is cooked and the water is absorbed, about 20 minutes.

Variation

Extra-Flavorful Rice

For more flavorful rice, use vegetable, chicken, or beef broth in place of the water.

Cheap Tip

We recommend buying rice in the bulk section, especially at a health-food store, where you'll find a large selection that includes varieties like brown rice, basmati, and jasmine. That way you can buy only as much as you need. Rice is cheaper at ethnic grocery stores but tends to be sold in large bags only. If you have enough cupboard space, you can buy a larger bag and always have some on hand. The rice will keep indefinitely, as long as it's tightly sealed.

COOKING TIME:
25 minutes

SERVES: *3 to 4*

EQUIPMENT:
liquid measuring cup, medium saucepan with lid, measuring cups

Don't Let This Happen to You

Burned rice is really difficult to scrub out of the bottom of a saucepan. When you cook rice, make sure the heat is as low as you can get it, and keep an eye on the saucepan to make sure there's still enough water in the bottom. If you hear a sizzling or popping sound, or if you smell something burning, that's a bad sign. Check the rice right away.

Black Beans and Rice

Black beans and rice is a basic, satisfying meal that you'll find yourself making over and over again. The leftovers keep well and actually get better with age (within reason, of course).

Basic Rice recipe (page 92)
4 slices bacon, diced
1 medium onion, peeled and diced
1 stalk celery, diced
2 medium garlic cloves, peeled and minced
1 small hot chile, such as jalapeño, seeded and minced (see tip)
2 (15 ounce/425 g) cans black beans, drained
1/2 cup (120 ml) water
Pinch of salt
Pinch of black pepper
Fresh Tomato Salsa (page 36) (optional)
Sour cream (optional)

1. Start cooking the rice, following the directions on page 92.
2. Heat a medium saucepan over medium heat. Add the bacon and fry it until it is as browned and crispy as you like it.
3. Using a fork, transfer the bacon to a plate, leaving the fat behind. Set the bacon aside at room temperature.
4. Add the onion and celery to the saucepan with the bacon fat. Sauté over medium heat, stirring occasionally, until the onion becomes translucent, about 4 minutes.
5. Add the garlic and hot chile; sauté 1 minute, stirring occasionally.
6. Add the black beans and 1/2 cup water; bring to a boil. Turn the heat to low, cover with the lid and simmer for 10 minutes.
7. Add the reserved bacon to the beans and stir to combine. Taste the beans to see how much salt and pepper you want to add. Serve with the rice, topping with Fresh Tomato Salsa and sour cream, if desired.

Variation

Vegetarian Black Beans and Rice

The high-protein combination of beans and rice is a popular vegetarian staple. To make a vegetarian version of this recipe, leave out the bacon and skip Steps 2 and 3. Fry the onion and celery in 2 teaspoons of vegetable oil instead of the bacon fat.

PREP TIME:
15 minutes

COOKING TIME:
25 to 30 minutes

SERVES: *4*

EQUIPMENT:
medium saucepan with lid, all-purpose knife, cutting board, fork, plate, large spoon, can opener, liquid measuring cup

Don't Let This Happen to You

We can't say this enough: Avoid getting juice from a hot chile in your eyes or on your face; it's really not a fun experience. Several hours after you've finished cooking, it's easy to forget that some of the chile juice got on your fingers. But if you happen to rub your face or eyes, you'll get a painful reminder.

Rice Pilaf with Cashews and Green Onion

This rice dish is especially nice to serve with Indian Chicken Curry (page 73) or Indian Potato and Cauliflower Curry (page 65). Don't be afraid of using cinnamon in a savory dish; it adds an exotic spiciness to the rice, but won't make it taste like dessert.

2 cups (475 ml) water
Pinch of salt
1 cup (180 g) long-grain white rice, such as basmati
1/3 cup (35 g) roughly chopped cashews (see Cheap Tip)
2 green onions, white and green parts, chopped
1/4 teaspoon ground cinnamon

1. Place 2 cups of water in a medium saucepan. Add a pinch of salt. Bring to a boil over high heat.
2. Add the rice, cover with the lid and turn the heat to low.
3. Simmer until the rice is cooked and the water is absorbed, about 20 minutes.
4. Fluff the rice with a fork. Add the cashews, green onion, and cinnamon and stir to combine (see tip).

PREP TIME: *3 minutes*

COOKING TIME: *25 minutes*

SERVES: *3 to 4*

EQUIPMENT: *liquid measuring cup, medium saucepan with lid, measuring cups, all-purpose knife, cutting board, large spoon or fork*

Variation

Nutty Rice Pilaf

Substitute pistachios or peanuts (or whatever nuts you have on hand) for the cashews.

Cheap Tip

If you buy cashews or other nuts from the bulk section, where they're cheaper, you may want to taste one first. (Ask a store employee if you can taste one for freshness; a reputable store will have no problem with that.) Packaged nuts list an expiration date, so you know how fresh they are. In the bulk section, there's no telling how long the nuts have been there.

Don't Let This Happen to You

If you're making the rice in advance, don't add the green onions or cashews until the last minute. Otherwise, the green onions will wilt and the cashews will soften.

The Easiest Couscous

Couscous is teeny, tiny pasta that doesn't need to be cooked—only rehydrated. The package instructions say to mix the couscous with boiling water, but you don't really need to. Use lukewarm water instead, and the couscous will still end up with the right texture.

1 cup (185 g) instant plain or whole-wheat couscous (see Cheap Tip)
1 tablespoon olive oil or vegetable oil
1/4 teaspoon salt
1 to 1 1/4 cups (235 to 295 ml) water

1. Place the couscous, oil, and salt in a medium bowl. Add 1 cup (235 ml) water (if you're using whole-wheat couscous, make that 1 1/4 cups [295 ml] water). Stir once with a fork.
2. Set the couscous aside for 15 minutes, or until it is rehydrated. Fluff with a fork. Serve at room temperature or chilled.

PREP TIME: *2 minutes*

RESTING TIME: *15 minutes*

SERVES: *2*

EQUIPMENT: *measuring cups and spoons, medium bowl, liquid measuring cup, fork*

Variation

The Easiest, Quickest Couscous

Place 1 cup (235 ml) of water in a small microwave-safe mug or bowl. Microwave on high until the water comes to a boil. (If you don't have a microwave, heat the water on the stove in a small saucepan.) Place the couscous, oil, and salt in a medium bowl and add the boiling water. Stir once with a fork and set aside for 5 minutes, or until the couscous is rehydrated.

Cheap Tip

Like most dry goods, couscous is much cheaper when you buy it from the bulk section—that way, you don't have to pay for any packaging. In the bulk section of a health-food store, you can choose between several types of couscous, including regular, organic, and whole-wheat. If you're shopping for couscous at the supermarket, look for boxes of it in the rice or pasta section. There you'll find flavors like garlic, herb, Parmesan, and curry.

Couscous with Peas and Parmesan

This speedy recipe is perfect for a busy day when you don't have much time or patience for cooking. First of all, you probably have most or all of the ingredients already on hand. (If you don't have frozen peas, use frozen corn or green beans instead.) Second, there's no need to use the stove because everything is heated in the microwave (why dirty a saucepan if you don't need to?). And third, this recipe is virtually impossible to screw up. Cooking doesn't get much easier than this.

1 cup (235 ml) water
1 cup (185 g) instant plain or whole-wheat couscous
1/2 cup (80 g) frozen peas (no need to thaw)
1 tablespoon butter
1/3 cup (35 g) grated or shredded Parmesan cheese
Large pinch of salt
Pinch of black pepper

1. Place the water in a microwave-safe mug or bowl. Microwave on high until the water comes to a boil. (If you don't have a microwave, heat the water on the stove in a small saucepan.)
2. Place the couscous in a medium bowl and add the boiling water. Stir once with a fork and set aside for 5 minutes.
3. Meanwhile, place the peas and butter in the same container that you used to boil the water. Microwave on high until the peas are warm and the butter is melted, about 1 minute.
4. Fluff the couscous with a fork. Add the peas and Parmesan cheese and stir to combine. Season with salt and pepper to taste.

PREP TIME:
7 minutes

COOKING TIME:
3 minutes

SERVES: *2 to 3*

EQUIPMENT:
liquid measuring cup, microwave-safe mug or bowl, microwave, measuring cups and spoons, medium bowl, fork

Soups

Let's face it: Cooking soup is not rocket science. Basically, you chop up some ingredients, throw them into a big pot with some liquid, and let the whole thing simmer on its own for a while. What could be simpler?

If you have a busy schedule, soup is a convenient option that will save you from having to make dinner every night. One batch of soup usually makes 4 to 6 servings, so you'll have enough to last you through the week. Don't worry—these aren't the kind of leftovers that you stow in the fridge and never touch again. In fact, a lot of soups get even better the second or third day.

Last but not least, soup is ultra-cheap. By using ingredients like onions, carrots, potatoes, and canned beans, you can feed yourself (or a crowd) with very little expense.

Comforting Chicken Soup

No matter when you try this soup for the first time, you'll wish you had made it sooner. It's that good—much better than any soup you would buy in a can. If you're feeling especially considerate, throw a batch together the next time your roommate gets sick (in the hope that he or she will return the favor someday).

1 tablespoon vegetable oil
1 medium onion, peeled and roughly chopped
2 stalks celery, washed and roughly chopped
1 large carrot, peeled or scrubbed and roughly chopped
1 medium garlic clove, peeled and minced
1 (32-ounce/1 liter) container chicken broth (4 cups)
2 sprigs fresh thyme (optional)
1 boneless skinless chicken breast, cut into 1/2-inch pieces (see Cheap Tip)
Pinch of salt
Pinch of black pepper

PREP TIME:
10 minutes

COOKING TIME:
30 to 40 minutes

SERVES: *2*

EQUIPMENT:
measuring cups and spoons, large saucepan with lid, all-purpose knife, cutting board, vegetable peeler, large spoon, fork

1. Heat the oil in a large saucepan over medium-high heat. Add the onion, celery, and carrot. Sauté, stirring occasionally, until the onion becomes translucent, 6 to 8 minutes.
2. Add the garlic, chicken broth, and thyme, if desired. Bring to a boil.
3. Turn the heat to low, cover with the lid, and simmer until the carrot is tender when pierced with a fork, about 15 minutes.
4. Add the chicken and simmer, covered, until it is no longer pink inside, 5 to 7 minutes.
5. Taste the soup to see how much salt and pepper you want to add.

Cheap Tip

This recipe calls for 1 boneless skinless chicken breast. If you like dark meat, you can substitute 2 boneless skinless chicken thighs. Thighs are usually cheaper per pound than breasts are. Because the thighs are sold in packages of six or more, you may want to freeze the remaining ones for your next chicken soup adventure.

Variations

Comforting Chicken Soup with Rice

To make the soup heartier, add 2 tablespoons of long-grain rice to the saucepan when you add the chicken broth. Make sure the rice cooks for at least 15 minutes.

Comforting Chicken Soup with Noodles

Use 1 cup (115 g) of egg noodles or short pasta such as bow ties or penne. Check the package directions to determine the cooking time, and add the pasta to the soup at the appropriate time. For instance, if the pasta is supposed to cook for 11 minutes, add it 6 minutes before you add the chicken.

Asian Dumpling Soup

We just can't get enough of potstickers—aka Asian dumplings—whether they're pan fried (page 91), steamed, or simmered in broth. This easy soup looks beautiful in the bowl, so it makes an ideal option for when you have company over for dinner.

1 (32 ounce/1 liter) container chicken or vegetable broth (see Cheap Tip on page 100)
8 to 12 frozen meat or vegetable Asian dumplings (no need to thaw)
1 to 3 teaspoons soy sauce
1 green onion, white and green parts, chopped
Pinch of red pepper flakes (optional)

1. Heat the broth in a large saucepan over medium-high heat.
2. Once the broth comes to a boil, add the frozen dumplings. Bring to a boil again and simmer until the dumplings are soft, about 5 minutes (see tip on page 100). Stir the soup occasionally to make sure the dumplings don't stick to the bottom of the saucepan or to each other.
3. Add 1 teaspoon of the soy sauce to the soup, then taste it to see if you want to add up to 2 teaspoons more.
4. Divide the soup and dumplings between two serving bowls. Top with the chopped green onion. If you like a bit of heat, add a sprinkle of red pepper flakes before serving.

PREP TIME:
2 minutes

COOKING TIME:
8 to 15 minutes

SERVES: *2*

EQUIPMENT:
large saucepan, large spoon or wooden spoon, measuring spoons, all-purpose knife, cutting board

(continued on following page)

(continued)

Variation

Asian Dumpling Soup with Chicken or Shrimp

Making this soup is a great way to use up leftovers. Add diced cooked chicken, or even shrimp, if you happen to have some. Slivers of bell pepper or sliced mushrooms would also enhance the look and flavor of the soup.

Cheap Tip

You have two basic options for buying chicken broth: canned broth or bouillon cubes. Bouillon cubes, which are cheaper, are concentrated and need to be rehydrated with hot water before using. (Follow the package directions.) Chicken broth made from bouillon cubes tends to be a bit salty and the flavor can be unpleasant. Canned chicken broth has a better flavor and is not as highly processed. Use the low-sodium version to keep the soup from getting too salty. You can always add more salt, but if there's too much to start with, it can be hard to tone it down.

Don't Let This Happen to You

If you overcook the soup, the dumplings will start to fall apart and their filling will escape. Take the saucepan off the heat as soon as the dumplings are heated all the way through.

Spicy Chili

Chili is a cheap dish that's perfect for feeding a crowd. For a special treat, offer toppings like shredded cheese, diced red onion, and sour cream. Freeze any leftover chili and use it later on to top stuffed potatoes (page 114) or eat with corn chips.

PREP TIME: *8 minutes*

COOKING TIME: *50 minutes*

SERVES: *4 to 6*

EQUIPMENT: *measuring cups and spoons, large saucepan with lid, all-purpose knife, cutting board, large spoon or wooden spoon, can opener, liquid measuring cup*

- 1 teaspoon vegetable oil
- 1 medium onion, peeled and diced
- 1 small hot chile, such as jalapeño, seeded and minced (see tip)
- 2 medium garlic cloves, peeled and minced
- 1 1/4 pounds (570 g) ground beef or turkey
- 1 1/2 tablespoons chili powder (see tip)
- 1 (28 ounce/785 g) can crushed tomatoes
- 1 cup (240 ml) water
- 1 (15 ounce/425 g) can black beans, drained (optional)
- Pinch of salt
- Pinch of black pepper

1. Heat the oil in a large saucepan over medium-high heat. Add the onion and sauté, stirring occasionally, until it becomes translucent, 4 to 5 minutes.
2. Add the chile, garlic, and ground meat. Break up the chunks of meat into smaller pieces. Cook until the meat is no longer pink, 5 to 7 minutes.
3. Add the chili powder and cook for 2 minutes, stirring occasionally.
4. Add the tomatoes and water and bring to a boil. Turn the heat to low, cover with the lid, and simmer for 30 minutes.
5. Add the black beans, if desired, and cook uncovered for 5 minutes.
6. Taste to see how much salt and pepper you want to add.

Don't Let This Happen to You

Make sure to buy the right kind of chili powder, or you might end up with a much hotter chili than you had expected. The chili powder we call for isn't a single spice: it's a mix of dried chiles, cumin, and other spices. If you're not sure you have the right kind, check the list of ingredients on the container before you buy it. If you buy straight chile powder, such as chipotle or ancho, it will be much, much hotter.

Likewise, watch out for the hot juices in the jalapeño, making sure not to touch your face or eyes after you've handled it.

Hearty Black Bean Soup

This creamy, filling bean soup is especially good with a dollop of sour cream on top. (But what soup isn't?)

4 slices bacon, diced
1 medium onion, peeled and diced
1 stalk celery, washed and diced
2 medium garlic cloves, peeled and minced
1 small hot chile, such as jalapeño, seeded and minced (see tip on page 103)
2 (15 ounce/425 g) cans black beans, drained
1 (14 ounce/415 ml) can chicken broth
Pinch of salt
Pinch of black pepper

PREP TIME: *15 minutes*

COOKING TIME: *45 minutes*

SERVES: *4*

EQUIPMENT: *large saucepan with lid, all-purpose knife, cutting board, fork, plate, large spoon, can opener, blender (optional), dish towel (optional)*

1. Heat a large saucepan over medium heat. Add the bacon and fry until it is as browned and crispy as you like it. Using a fork, transfer the bacon to a plate, leaving the fat behind in the saucepan. Set the bacon aside at room temperature.
2. Add the onion and celery to the saucepan. Sauté over medium heat, stirring occasionally, until the onion becomes translucent, about 4 minutes.
3. Add the garlic and hot chile; sauté 1 minute, stirring occasionally.
4. Add the black beans and chicken broth. Cover with the lid, turn the heat to low, and simmer for 30 minutes.
5. Now you have a choice: You can either add the bacon back to the saucepan and eat the soup as is, or, if you like a smoother soup, you can puree a few cups of it in the blender, add it back to the saucepan, and then add the bacon.
6. Taste the soup to see how much salt and pepper you want to add.

Variation

Vegetarian Black Bean Soup

To make a vegetarian version of this recipe, leave out the bacon and skip Step 1. Fry the onion and celery in 2 teaspoons of vegetable oil instead of the bacon fat. Substitute vegetable broth for the chicken broth.

Don't Let This Happen to You

When you blend a soup, protect yourself from the hot liquid by never filling the blender more than 2/3 full. (Blend the soup in batches if it doesn't all fit in the blender at once.) Always use the blender lid, and place a dish towel on top of it to block any spray.

Watch out for jalapeños—they look so small and cute, but the juice they harbor inside can really sting if it gets on your skin or in your eyes. Make sure to wash your hands well with soap and water after mincing the chile for this recipe, and avoid touching your face.

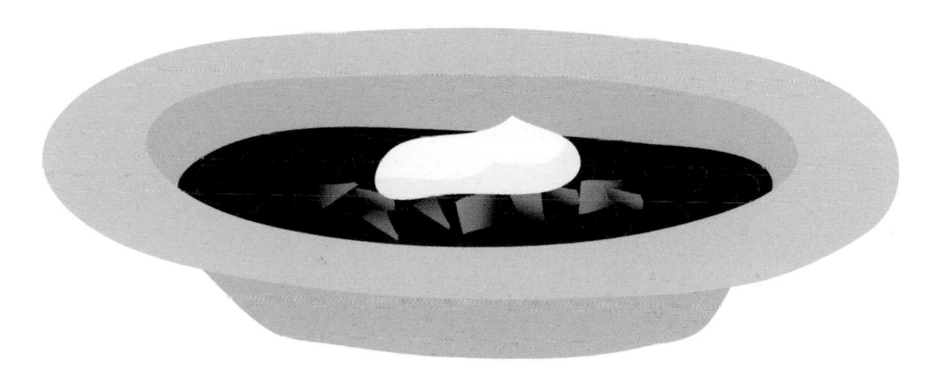

Lentil and Smoked Sausage Soup

As with all bean and legume soups, the flavor of this lentil soup gets better overnight, which means that it makes for great leftovers. We like to top each serving with a sprinkle of red wine vinegar and a dollop of sour cream.

1 tablespoon vegetable oil
1 medium onion, peeled and diced
2 carrots, scrubbed or peeled and diced
2 stalks celery, washed and diced
2 medium garlic cloves, peeled and minced
1 1/2 cups (300 g) dried lentils, picked over (see tip)
2 sprigs fresh thyme (optional)
6 cups (1.5 liters) water
12 to 16 ounces (340 to 455 g) fully cooked smoked sausage of your choice, sliced into rounds
Large pinch of salt
Large pinch of black pepper

1. Heat the oil in a large saucepan over medium-high heat. Add the onion, carrot, and celery. Sauté, stirring occasionally, until the onion becomes translucent, 6 to 8 minutes.
2. Add the garlic, lentils, and thyme, if desired. Add the water and bring to a boil.
3. Turn the heat to low, cover with the lid, and simmer until the vegetables and lentils are soft, about 1 hour.
4. Add the sausage and simmer for another 15 minutes.
5. Taste the soup to see how much salt and pepper you want to add.

PREP TIME:
20 minutes

COOKING TIME:
1 hour, 40 minutes

SERVES *4*

EQUIPMENT:
measuring cups and spoons, large saucepan with lid, all-purpose knife, cutting board, vegetable peeler, large spoon or wooden spoon, plate, liquid measuring cup

Variation

Vegetarian Lentil Soup

To make this soup vegetarian, simply leave out the smoked sausage and skip Step 4.

Don't Let This Happen to You

When you cook with dried legumes such as lentils or split peas, it's a good idea to spread them out on a plate and give them a quick look over before you put them in the pot. Pebbles seem to find their way into lentils. We have no idea why this is, but we always seem to find at least one. Take a minute to make sure they're all gone, and your teeth will be very grateful.

Creamy Corn and Potato Soup

This rich, velvety soup is not as thick as a chowder, so you can prepare it at any time of year. It's especially good in the summertime, when you can use fresh corn instead of frozen (just cut the kernels off the ears of corn before adding to the soup).

2 strips bacon, diced (see Cheap Tip)
1 small onion, peeled and chopped
1 medium russet potato, peeled and cut into 1/2-inch pieces
4 cups (480 g) frozen corn, divided (no need to thaw)
3 cups (710 ml) chicken broth
1 1/2 cups (355 ml) half-and-half
1/4 teaspoon salt
Large pinch of black pepper

1. In a medium saucepan over medium-high heat, fry the bacon until it is crisp, stirring occasionally, about 5 minutes.
2. Lower the heat to medium and add the onion. Cook, stirring occasionally, until the onion is translucent, about 3 minutes.
3. Add the potato and 3 cups (360 g) of the corn. Cook 3 minutes, stirring occasionally.
4. Add the chicken broth and bring to a boil. Turn the heat to low, cover with the lid, and simmer until the potato is tender when pierced with a fork, about 10 minutes.
5. Transfer the soup to a blender. Cover the lid with a dish towel, and puree the soup until it is smooth, about 15 seconds.
6. Return the soup to the saucepan and add the remaining 1 cup (120 g) corn. Add the half-and-half, salt, and pepper. Heat thoroughly, but do not bring to a boil.

PREP TIME:
10 minutes

COOKING TIME:
35 minutes

SERVES: *4 to 6*

EQUIPMENT:
medium saucepan with lid, all-purpose knife, cutting board, large spoon, vegetable peeler, measuring cups and spoons, liquid measuring cup, fork, blender, dish towel

Cheap Tip

You'll probably have several strips of leftover bacon after you make this recipe. Put the bacon package in a freezer bag and stick it in the freezer for up to 2 or 3 months. Bacon is much easier to cut up when it's frozen, anyway.

Cucumber-Buttermilk Soup

Chilled, made-in-the-blender soups like this one are perfect for summer, when you don't really feel like heating up the kitchen. The cucumber and buttermilk make this soup refreshing, whereas the green onion and garlic add a little bit of a kick. If you want a really tangy soup, substitute 1/2 cup (120 ml) of plain yogurt for half of the buttermilk.

2 medium cucumbers
2 green onions, white and green parts, chopped
1 medium garlic clove, peeled
1 cup (240 ml) buttermilk
Large pinch of salt
Large pinch of black pepper

1. Peel the cucumbers and cut the tips off both ends. Cut into large chunks and place in the blender.
2. Add the green onion and garlic to the blender. Add the buttermilk, salt, and pepper.
3. Put the lid on and blend for 10 to 20 seconds. Check the soup to see if you like the texture; if not, keep blending until it is as smooth as you like it. If it seems that the cucumbers are not getting incorporated, stop the blender occasionally and stir with a large spoon or rubber spatula. Eat the soup right away, or chill until ready to serve.

PREP TIME:
6 to 8 minutes

SERVES: *4*

EQUIPMENT:
vegetable peeler, all-purpose knife, cutting board, blender, liquid measuring cup, large spoon or rubber spatula

Chilled Gazpacho

When it's too hot to cook, turn to gazpacho (pronounced gahz-PAH-choh), a refreshing tomato soup that we've filled with tiny, colorful bits of cucumber, red onion, and bell pepper. There's no cooking required, just some chopping to prep the vegetables and then a few whirls in the blender.

PREP TIME:
15 to 25 minutes

CHILLING TIME:
1 hour or longer

SERVES: *4*

EQUIPMENT:
paring knife, all-purpose knife, cutting board, blender, large bowl, vegetable peeler, small spoon, measuring cups and spoons, large spoon, liquid measuring cup, fork, plastic wrap

2 pounds (900 g) ripe tomatoes (about 4 medium) (see Cheap Tip)
1 medium cucumber, peeled
1 medium red onion, peeled
1 red or yellow bell pepper, halved and seeded
6 medium garlic cloves, peeled
3 tablespoons chopped fresh parsley
1/4 cup (60 ml) white or red wine vinegar
1/2 lime, or more to taste
1 1/2 teaspoons salt, or more to taste
1/2 teaspoon black pepper
1/2 cup (120 ml) olive oil

1. Using a paring knife, cut the cores out of the tomatoes. To seed the tomatoes, cut them in half crosswise and squeeze out the seeds into the trash or garbage disposal. With an all-purpose knife, cut the tomatoes into large chunks and transfer to the blender. Pulse until they are broken up into small pieces, about 10 pulses. Pour out into a large bowl, leaving about 1 cup of the tomatoes in the bottom of the blender.
2. To seed the cucumber, cut it in half lengthwise and scoop out the seeds with a small spoon. Chop the cucumber, red onion, bell pepper, and garlic. Transfer 1 cup of the chopped vegetables to the large bowl to join the tomatoes; place the rest in the blender.
3. Pulse until the vegetables are chopped into small pieces, about 20 pulses. (You may need to stop the blender periodically to stir the mixture with a large spoon.) Transfer the vegetables to the large bowl.
4. Add the parsley and vinegar to the bowl. Squeeze the lime half over the bowl, using a fork to poke the flesh and get more juice out. Pick out any seeds with a spoon.
5. Add the salt and pepper and stir well, tasting the soup to see if it needs more salt or lime juice.
6. Cover the bowl with plastic wrap and chill the soup thoroughly, at least 1 hour. Just before serving, stir in the olive oil.

Cheap Tip

Tomatoes are at their cheapest and juiciest in the summer months. You'll find the sweetest, ripest ones at a farmers market or a roadside vegetable stand. Look for blemish-free tomatoes that seem heavy for their size. Try some fun varieties that you wouldn't normally find at a supermarket, such as Cherokee Purple, Green Zebra, or Mr. Stripey.

7 Veggies and Salads

Are you the type of person who likes to plan ahead and buy a month's worth of groceries all in one shopping trip? That strategy might work well for pantry items, but fresh produce doesn't last for a month. Lettuce in particular doesn't benefit from sitting in the refrigerator for a week or longer.

If you want to minimize your trips to the grocery store, buy all of your staples at once, but wait until the last minute to pick up salad greens and other fresh vegetables. That way, you won't be wasting your money on beautiful produce that ends up turning to sludge in your refrigerator's vegetable bin.

Whether you're shopping at a grocery store or a farmers market, there are certain things you should look for when buying fresh produce. Think crisp, not wilted; look for brightly colored skins, not brown or spotted ones. Needless to say, avoid anything that looks slimy or has liquid seeping from it.

Once you've picked out the best vegetables you can find, turn to these recipes for quick, simple ways to prepare them.

Steamed Vegetables

Steaming vegetables couldn't be easier. The only ingredients you need are the vegetables themselves, and perhaps a little salt or pepper sprinkled on them once they've finished cooking.

For the steaming process, you have two main choices: on the stove or in the microwave. To steam vegetables on the stovetop, use a metal basket steamer, the kind that opens up like a flower. Open the steamer and place it, "petals" facing up, in the bottom of a saucepan. Add an inch of water to the saucepan and bring to a boil. You should not be able to see any water coming up through the bottom of the steamer.

Cut the vegetables in pieces that are roughly the same size, so they will cook evenly. Place them inside the steamer and cover the saucepan tightly with a lid.

Deciding when the vegetables are done cooking is a bit subjective. Some people like their vegetables to be very crunchy; others want something akin to baby food. And most people like their vegetables somewhere in between. Vegetables like broccoli and cauliflower may only need 5 minutes to get tender, whereas denser vegetables like potatoes may take up to 35 minutes to cook all the way through. Check the vegetables often as they cook, poking with a fork and tasting occasionally, and you'll be able to get them just the way you like them.

To steam vegetables in the microwave, place them in a microwave-safe dish and cover with plastic wrap. Vegetables like zucchini, asparagus, spinach, cauliflower, broccoli, and green beans don't need any extra water in the dish. For denser vegetables like potatoes, carrots, or winter squash, add a few teaspoons of water to the bottom of the dish.

Microwave the vegetables on high for 2 minutes, then open the microwave to check on them. Be careful when you lift up the plastic wrap; open the side that's facing away from you, and use a towel to protect your hand from escaping steam. If the vegetables aren't tender yet, continue cooking in 30-second increments until they are. Keep in mind that the vegetables will continue cooking after the microwave has stopped, especially if the plastic wrap is still covering them.

Perfect Corn on the Cob

Get out the dental floss—it's time to sink your choppers into some sweet, juicy corn on the cob.

4 large ears fresh corn (see Cheap Tip)
Butter, or one of the butter variations
Pinch of salt

1. Fill a large saucepan with at least 2 quarts (2 liters) of water. Bring to a boil over high heat.
2. Peel the husks off of the ears of corn and pull off all the silk.
3. Add the ears of corn to the boiling water and cook for 6 to 8 minutes, or until the kernels are tender.
4. Using tongs or 2 forks, take the ears of corn out of the water. Serve each ear with butter and a sprinkle of salt.

PREP TIME:
5 minutes

COOKING TIME:
6 to 8 minutes

SERVES: *4*

EQUIPMENT:
large saucepan, tongs or 2 forks

Garlic Butter

Mince 1 medium garlic clove and mix with 4 tablespoons (1/2 stick) of softened butter.

Chili-Lime Butter

Mix the juice from half a lime with a large pinch of chili powder and 4 tablespoons (1/2 stick) of softened butter.

Cheap Tip

Summer is the best time of year to make corn on the cob, because corn is much more plentiful, and therefore cheaper. Farmers markets offer especially good deals on corn during the summer. Whether you're buying corn in the husk or already shucked, look for ears that are plump, not shriveled, and show no sign of mold or rot. Corn loses its sweetness quickly once it's been picked, so try to use it right away. At other times of the year, you can buy packaged fresh or frozen corn ears, but they won't have as much flavor as the fresh-from-the-garden version.

Buttery Glazed Carrots

The loud crunch of raw carrots is a good stress reliever, but there's also something to be said for tender, not-so-noisy cooked carrots, especially when they're lightly coated with a glaze of melted butter and brown sugar.

PREP TIME:
5 minutes

COOKING TIME:
12 minutes

SERVES: *2*

EQUIPMENT:
vegetable peeler, all-purpose knife, cutting board, measuring spoons, small saucepan with lid, liquid measuring cup, fork

1/2 pound carrots (225 g) (about 4 medium), peeled or scrubbed (see Cheap Tip)
1 tablespoon butter
1 tablespoon packed light or dark brown sugar
Pinch of salt
1/4 cup (60 ml) water

1. Trim the stem end off of each carrot. Cut the carrots into 1/4-inch-thick rounds.
2. Combine the carrots, butter, brown sugar, and salt in a small saucepan. Add the water, cover with the lid, and bring to a simmer over medium heat.
3. Simmer until the carrots are almost tender when pierced with a fork, about 7 minutes.
4. Uncover and continue simmering until the liquid thickens to a glaze and the carrots get syrupy, about 2 minutes.

Cheap Tip

Carrots, like most vegetables, are remarkably inexpensive. For a little more money, you can buy carrots that still have their greens attached; these carrots can be fresher and sweeter than the ones sold in plastic bags. Make sure to twist the greens off right away when you get home, or better yet, ask someone who works at the supermarket to remove them for you.

Mashed Potatoes

Don't worry about mashing every last bit of potato; chunky mashed potatoes seem more homemade than the perfectly smooth ones do. If you're trying to decide how much to make, remember that one medium potato will feed one person as a side dish.

4 medium russet or other baking potatoes (see Cheap Tip on page 113)
2 tablespoons butter, softened
1/4 to 1/2 cup (60 to 120 ml) milk or cream
1/4 teaspoon salt
Pinch of black pepper

1. Peel the potatoes and cut them into 1-inch pieces. Place them in a large saucepan and add just enough water to cover.
2. Bring the potatoes to a boil over high heat. Lower the heat to medium and simmer the potatoes until they are tender when pierced with a fork, 12 to 14 minutes.
3. Drain the potatoes and return to the saucepan. Mash with a fork until all of the big chunks are broken up.

PREP TIME:
10 minutes

COOKING TIME:
25 minutes

SERVES: *4*

EQUIPMENT:
vegetable peeler, all-purpose knife, cutting board, large saucepan, fork, colander, measuring spoon, liquid measuring cup

4. Add the butter to the potatoes and mash to combine.
5. Add 1/4 cup of the milk to the potatoes and stir. Add more milk as necessary to give the potatoes a fluffy consistency.
6. Add the salt and pepper. Taste the mashed potatoes to see if you want to add more seasoning or butter.

Variations

Microwave Mashed Potatoes

You can easily microwave the potatoes instead of cooking them on the stove. Just peel them, cut them up, place them on a microwave-safe plate, and microwave on high until they are tender when pierced with a fork. Transfer to a large bowl before mashing.

Extra-Rich Mashed Potatoes

When you add the butter to the potatoes, throw in 1/4 cup (2 ounces/60 g) of cream cheese as well. The cream cheese will add creaminess and a bit of a tang.

Garlic Mashed Potatoes

While the potatoes are cooking, melt 2 teaspoons of butter in a small skillet over medium heat. Add 1 to 2 medium cloves of minced garlic to the skillet and simmer until slightly golden, about 1 to 2 minutes. Add the garlic to the potatoes at the same time as the butter.

Cheap Tip

The cheapest way to buy potatoes is by the bag. If you want larger potatoes, such as for stuffed potatoes (page 114), you may need to buy the potatoes individually. In either case, make sure the potatoes are still firm and not sprouting or turning green.

Stuffed Potato with Chili and Cheese

Looking for a creative way to use up leftovers? Consider putting them on top of a baked potato. You don't even have to fire up the oven to make one—just the microwave.

1 large russet or other baking potato
1/2 cup (120 ml) purchased chili or Spicy Chili (page 101), heated
1/4 cup (1 ounce/30 g) shredded cheddar cheese

1. Wash the potato and pierce it several times with a fork.
2. Wrap the potato in a paper towel and microwave on high until it's tender when pierced with a fork, 4 to 6 minutes.
3. Carefully remove the hot potato from the paper towel and slit it down the middle.
4. Top the potato with hot chili and cheese.

PREP TIME: *2 minutes*

COOKING TIME: *4 to 6 minutes*

SERVES: *1*

EQUIPMENT: *fork, paper towel, knife, grater*

Variation

Stuffed Potato with Chive Cream Cheese

Top the potato with a dollop of Chive Cream Cheese (page 53).

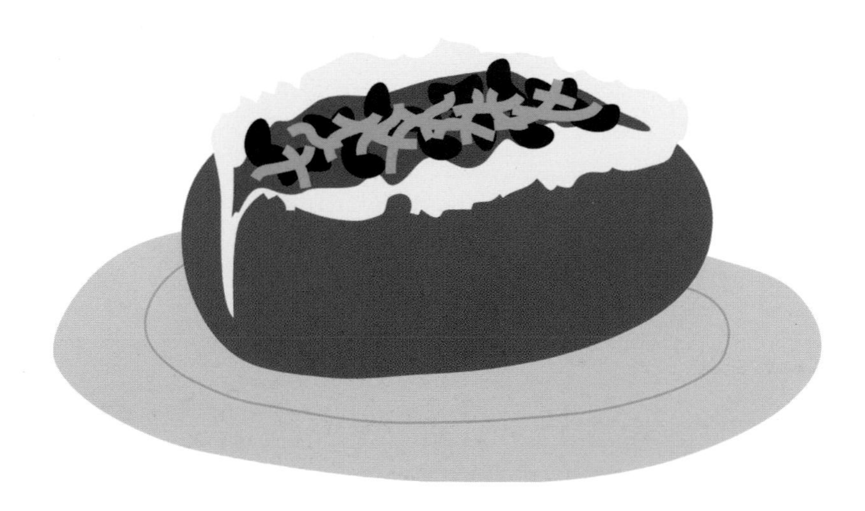

Green Beans with Almonds

Leave the green beans whole because they look nicer that way (it also takes less time to prepare them).

1 tablespoon butter
8 ounces (1/2 pound/230 g) green beans, washed, stems snapped off
1 tablespoon slivered or sliced almonds
Pinch of salt
Pinch of black pepper

1. Melt the butter in a large skillet over medium-high heat.
2. Add the green beans and sauté, stirring occasionally, until they are tender but still crisp, 5 to 8 minutes.
3. Add the almonds and sauté for 1 minute.
4. Season with salt and pepper (see tip).

PREP TIME:
3 minutes

COOKING TIME:
12 minutes

SERVES: *2*

EQUIPMENT:
measuring spoons, large skillet, fork

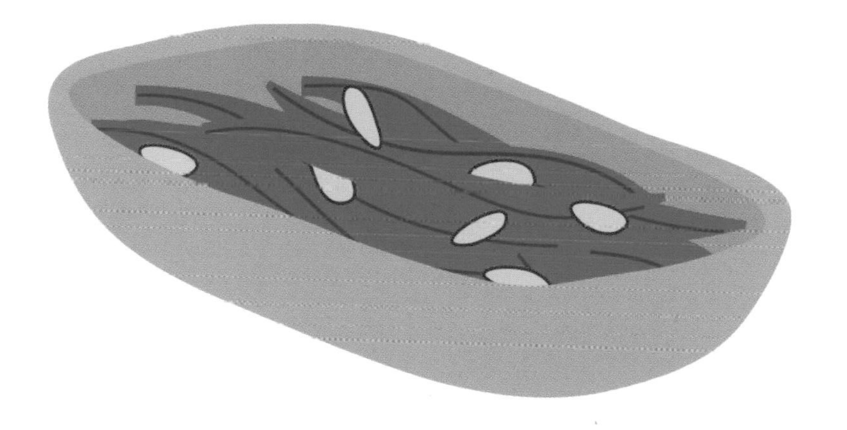

Don't Let This Happen to You

One of us (who shall remain nameless) tends to be a little overzealous with the salt shaker, and sometimes her dishes turn out to be too salty. To prevent this from happening to you, add a little bit of salt at a time, and keep tasting after each addition. Better to under-season than to have people complain that your dish is too salty.

Asparagus with Browned Butter

Browned butter is just what it sounds like—butter that's been melted until it turns brown and toasty. It's one of the easiest sauces you can make, and it goes well with nearly any vegetable. It's also superb on Cream of Wheat.

1 bunch fresh asparagus, rinsed (see Cheap Tip)
2 tablespoons water
2 tablespoons butter
Pinch of salt
Pinch of black pepper

1. Cut or snap any tough white ends off the bottoms of the asparagus.
2. Heat a large skillet over medium heat. Add the asparagus and water.
3. Cover the skillet with the lid and cook until asparagus is tender but not mushy, 5 to 7 minutes. The thinner the asparagus spears are, the less time they will take.
4. With tongs or 2 forks, transfer the asparagus from the skillet to a plate. Cover the plate with foil to keep warm. Pour any water out of the skillet.
5. Place the skillet over high heat. Add the butter and heat, stirring constantly, until it melts and just starts to turn brown and bubbly, about 3 minutes.
6. Remove the foil from the plate, and pour the browned butter over the asparagus. Season with salt and pepper.

PREP TIME:
2 minutes

COOKING TIME:
10 minutes

SERVES: *2*

EQUIPMENT:
all-purpose knife, cutting board, large skillet with lid, measuring spoons, tongs or 2 forks, plate, aluminum foil, large spoon or wooden spoon

Don't Let This Happen to You

Toasty browned butter can quickly turn into burned butter if you don't keep an eye on it. As soon as the butter smells nutty and starts to turn brown, take it off the heat and pour it over the asparagus. Otherwise, the heat from the skillet will continue to cook (and possibly burn) it.

Cheap Tip

The price for asparagus varies considerably, depending on what time of year you buy it. As with most vegetables, it's best to buy it in season, which for asparagus means March through May. Look for spears that are firm—not shriveled or slimy. The buds at the top should not be blooming.

Basic Green Salad

Toss the vinaigrette with the salad right before you serve it.

2 tablespoons vinegar of your choice
1/3 cup (80 ml) vegetable oil or olive oil
Pinch of sugar (optional)
Pinch of salt
Pinch of pepper
1 (8 ounce/230 g) bag washed salad greens, such as romaine or arugula

PREP TIME: *6 minutes*

SERVES: *4*

EQUIPMENT: *measuring spoons, large bowl, liquid measuring cup, fork or jar with tight-fitting lid, 2 spoons*

1. You have two choices for mixing the dressing:

Choice A: Place the vinegar in a large bowl. Slowly drizzle the oil into the bowl as you stir with a fork. Add a pinch of sugar, if desired, and salt and pepper to taste. Add the greens to the bowl and toss with the dressing.

Choice B: Place the vinegar, oil, and sugar in a small jar. Screw the lid on tight and shake until combined. Add the salt and pepper. Place the greens in a large bowl, pour the dressing over them, and toss to combine.

Caesar Salad with Garlic Croutons

To make a decent Caesar salad, you don't need to make the dressing from scratch, but homemade croutons do make a huge difference.

5 to 6 slices of bread, such as sourdough or baguette (see Cheap Tip)
5 to 6 tablespoons butter
1 medium garlic clove, peeled and minced
Large pinch of salt
Pinch of black pepper
5 ounces (140 g) romaine lettuce
3 tablespoons bottled Caesar dressing
2 tablespoons Parmesan cheese (optional)

1. Preheat the oven to 350 degrees F (180 degrees C).
2. Slice the crusts off the bread and cut the bread into 1-inch cubes. There's no need to be exact; just make the cubes roughly the same size.
3. Place the butter in a medium microwave-safe bowl. Microwave on high until it melts.
4. Add the bread cubes to the bowl with the melted butter. Add the garlic, salt, and pepper, using a fork to toss.
5. Spread the bread cubes on a baking sheet and place in the oven. Bake until the croutons are crispy, about 20 minutes. Remove from the oven and let cool for 5 minutes.
6. Place the romaine lettuce in a large bowl. Add the Caesar dressing and Parmesan cheese, if desired. Top with the croutons. Using 2 spoons, toss gently.

PREP TIME:
5 minutes

BAKING TIME:
20 minutes

SERVES: *2*

EQUIPMENT:
all-purpose knife, cutting board, measuring spoons, medium microwave-safe bowl, microwave, fork, baking sheet, large bowl, 2 spoons

Cheap Tip

If you have some bread that will go stale before you have a chance to use it, don't throw it away—make croutons instead.

Spinach Salad with Warm Bacon Dressing

This impressive, restaurant-style salad is surprisingly easy to prepare.

2 slices bacon, diced
2 tablespoons diced red onion
3 tablespoons red wine vinegar
1 tablespoon vegetable oil
Pinch of salt
Pinch of black pepper
6 ounces (170 g) washed spinach (see Cheap Tip)

1. Heat a small skillet over medium heat. Fry the bacon until it's crisp, about 5 minutes.
2. Using a fork, transfer the bacon from the skillet to a plate. Set aside at room temperature. Leave the bacon fat in the skillet.
3. Add the red onion to the bacon fat and sauté over medium heat until soft, about 1 minute. Turn the heat off.
4. Add the vinegar and oil to the skillet and stir with a fork. Season with salt and pepper.
5. Place the spinach in a large bowl. Add the warm bacon dressing and reserved bacon and toss to combine.

PREP TIME:
5 minutes

COOKING TIME:
7 minutes

SERVES: *2*

EQUIPMENT:
small skillet, all-purpose knife, cutting board, fork, plate, measuring spoons, large bowl, 2 spoons

Cheap Tip

Bagged spinach is more expensive than loose spinach, but its added convenience may be well worth the extra cost. Loose spinach still has a lot of mud clinging to it and needs several careful rinses to get clean. Bagged spinach has already been thoroughly washed, but you can rinse it again if you want.

Greek Salad

This salad is especially easy to make because it doesn't need to be tossed—just spread out on a plate.

PREP TIME: *10 minutes*

SERVES: *2*

EQUIPMENT: *large plate, all-purpose knife, cutting board, paring knife, small bowl, measuring cups and spoons, fork*

4 to 5 ounces (110 to 140 g) torn romaine lettuce
1/2 small red onion, very thinly sliced
1 medium tomato, cored and cut into thin wedges
10 to 12 black olives
1/4 cup (30 g) crumbled feta cheese
1 1/2 tablespoons balsamic or red wine vinegar
3 tablespoons olive oil
Pinch of salt
Pinch of black pepper

1. Place the lettuce on a large plate.
2. Separate the red onion slices into rings and place on the lettuce. Top with the tomato wedges, olives, and feta cheese.
3. In a small bowl, combine the vinegar, olive oil, salt, and pepper, stirring with a fork to combine. Drizzle as much dressing over the salad as you like and serve.

Variation

Lemony Greek Salad

To add more tang to the dressing, substitute an equal amount of lemon juice for the vinegar.

Don't Let This Happen to You

Don't use canned black California olives for this salad because they won't have the right kind of flavor. (Those olives are made for pizza and relish trays.) Use the cured Greek-type olives instead, such as kalamata. But beware: Sometimes the pits are still inside. You can leave the olives unpitted; just make sure to warn anyone else who's eating the salad.

Classic Coleslaw

Most of the ingredients for this salad are ones that you probably already have on hand; just pick up a bag of fresh coleslaw mix from the produce section, and you're set.

1/2 cup (110 g) mayonnaise
3 tablespoons vinegar (any kind)
2 teaspoons sugar
1/4 teaspoon salt
Large pinch of black pepper
1 (8 ounce/225 g) bag coleslaw mix or shredded cabbage

1. Place the mayonnaise, vinegar, sugar, salt, and pepper in a large bowl, stirring with a large spoon to combine.
2. Add the coleslaw mix or shredded cabbage to the dressing and stir to combine.
3. Taste the coleslaw and see if you want to add more vinegar, sugar, salt, and/or black pepper.

PREP TIME:
5 minutes

SERVES: *3 to 4*

EQUIPMENT:
measuring cups and spoons, large bowl, large spoon or wooden spoon

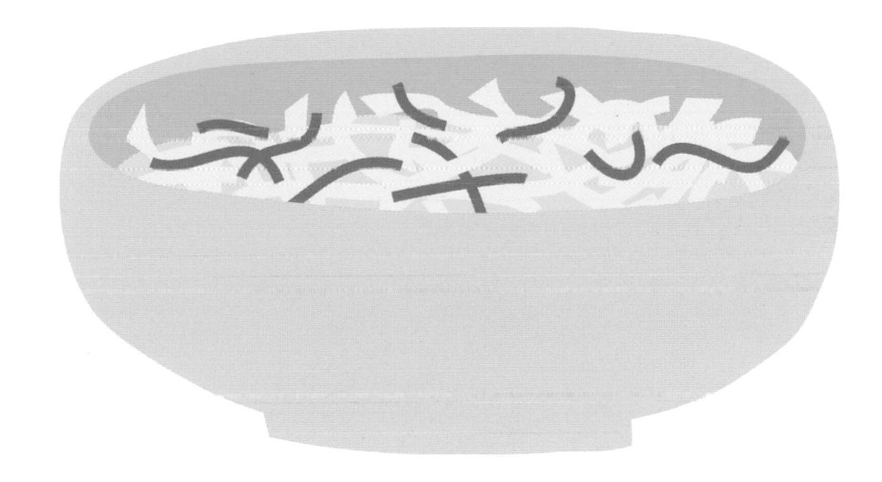

Chunky Potato Salad

We recommend using red new potatoes for this salad because you won't have to bother peeling them. They also hold up better in the salad because they're waxy potatoes; russet and other starchy baking potatoes tend to crumble.

1 (2 pound/900 g) bag red new potatoes, washed
2 stalks celery, washed and chopped
1 small red onion, peeled and diced
2 tablespoons sweet pickle relish
3/4 to 1 cup (165 to 220 g) mayonnaise
1 teaspoon yellow mustard
1/4 teaspoon salt
Large pinch of black pepper

1. Place the potatoes in a large saucepan and cover with water.
2. Bring to a boil over high heat. Lower the heat to medium, and cook the potatoes until they are tender when pierced with a fork, 10 to 20 minutes (see tip).
3. Once the potatoes are cool enough to handle, quarter them, leaving the skins on.
4. In a large bowl, combine the celery, red onion, relish, 3/4 cup (165 g) of the mayonnaise, mustard, salt, and pepper.
5. Add the potatoes to the bowl and stir gently to combine.
6. If you like a creamier potato salad, add another 1/4 cup (55 g) mayonnaise. Chill the salad until ready to serve.

PREP TIME:
10 minutes

COOKING TIME:
30 to 45 minutes

SERVES: *4 to 6*

EQUIPMENT:
large saucepan, fork, large bowl, all-purpose knife, cutting board, measuring cups and spoons, large spoon

Don't Let This Happen to You

You'll know you've overcooked the potatoes if they start falling apart in the boiling water. Check often to see if they are tender by piercing with a fork; it should go through the potato smoothly but not make the potato fall apart. The cooking time will vary, depending on the size of the potatoes and their freshness.

Cucumber-Buttermilk Salad

This light, refreshing salad makes a perfect side dish for a summer barbecue.

2 medium cucumbers
2 green onions, white and green parts, chopped
1 medium garlic clove, peeled and minced
1 cup (240 ml) buttermilk
Large pinch of salt
Large pinch of black pepper

1. Peel the cucumbers (see tip) and cut the tips off both ends. Slice the cucumbers as thinly as you can. Place them in a large bowl.
2. Add the green onion and garlic to the bowl. Add the buttermilk, salt, and pepper. Stir to combine.
3. At this point, you can either eat the salad right away or let it set in the refrigerator for several hours, giving the cucumbers time to soften.

PREP TIME:
8 minutes

SERVES: *4*

EQUIPMENT:
vegetable peeler, all-purpose knife, cutting board, large bowl, liquid measuring cup, wooden spoon or large spoon

Don't Let This Happen to You

If you use English hothouse cucumbers, you can save a step and leave the skins on. The green color will brighten up the salad. Don't think of leaving the skins on regular waxy cucumbers, however. These skins are tough and bitter and can leave a bad taste in your mouth for days.

Tomato, Mozzarella, and Basil Salad

Once you make this salad for the first time, you'll never have to refer to this recipe again—it's that easy.

2 large ripe tomatoes
1/4 cup (5 g) fresh basil leaves
8 ounces (225 g) fresh mozzarella (see tip)
Pinch of salt
Pinch of black pepper
1 tablespoon olive oil

1. Cut the cores out of the tomatoes and slice them thinly crosswise. Lay the tomato slices in a single layer on a plate.
2. Put a basil leaf or two on top of each tomato slice.
3. If you're using large mozzarella balls, cut them into thin round slices. If you're using small ones, cut them in half. Lay the cheese slices on top of the tomato slices.
4. Sprinkle the salad with salt and pepper. Drizzle with the olive oil.

PREP TIME:
8 minutes

SERVES: *4*

EQUIPMENT:
paring knife, all-purpose knife, cutting board, plate, measuring spoons

Don't Let This Happen to You

Don't buy the squeaky pizza kind of mozzarella; it doesn't have enough flavor on its own for this type of recipe. Look for fresh mozzarella cheese at Italian markets or health-food stores. You want to get the water-packed kind, in either large or small balls.

Asian Noodle Salad

Toasting the sesame seeds is optional—it adds a nuttier flavor and only takes a few minutes. To toast the seeds, heat a small skillet over medium heat. Place the sesame seeds in the skillet and toast, stirring often, until the seeds are golden in color and have a pronounced sesame fragrance.

1 (12 ounce/340 g) package soba or udon noodles
2 green onions, white and green parts, thinly sliced
1 1/2 teaspoons minced fresh ginger (bottled is OK)
1 medium garlic clove, peeled and minced
2 tablespoons rice vinegar
2 tablespoons soy sauce
1 tablespoon vegetable oil
1/4 cup (40 g) frozen peas (no need to thaw)
1 tablespoon sesame seeds (toasted, if desired)

1. Fill a large saucepan with at least 3 quarts of water. Bring to a boil over high heat.
2. Add the noodles and cook according to package directions.
3. While the noodles are cooking, prep the rest of the ingredients. Place the green onion, ginger, garlic, vinegar, soy sauce, vegetable oil, and peas in a large bowl.
4. Drain the noodles, and rinse with cold water. Add the noodles to the bowl and mix well. Add the sesame seeds, toasting them first, if desired.

PREP TIME:
10 minutes

COOKING TIME:
10 minutes

SERVES: *4*

EQUIPMENT:
large saucepan, all-purpose knife, cutting board, measuring cups and spoons, large bowl, colander, large spoon

Variation

Vegetable Asian Noodle Salad

To add more color and flavor to the salad, throw in shredded carrot, thinly sliced bell pepper, or thinly sliced cabbage.

Couscous and Vegetable Salad

This easy vegan main course salad responds well to any leftovers you might want to add to it.

1 cup (240 ml) water
1 cup (185 g) instant plain or whole-wheat couscous
1 small red onion, peeled and minced
1 small carrot, scrubbed or peeled and grated
1/2 medium cucumber, peeled and diced
1 medium tomato, cored and diced
1/4 cup (5 g) chopped fresh basil or parsley
3 tablespoons vinegar (any kind)
1/2 cup (120 ml) vegetable oil
Pinch of sugar
Pinch of salt
Pinch of black pepper

1. Place the water in a small microwave-safe mug or bowl. Microwave on high until the water comes to a boil. (If you don't have a microwave, heat the water on the stove in a small saucepan.)
2. Place the couscous in a large bowl and add the boiling water. Stir once with a fork and set aside for 5 minutes, or until the couscous is rehydrated.
3. Add the red onion, carrot, cucumber, tomato, and basil to the couscous. Stir to combine.
4. Place the vinegar in a small bowl. With a fork, gradually mix in the oil. Add the sugar, salt, and pepper.
5. Pour the dressing over the couscous mixture and toss to combine. Taste the salad to see if you want to add more salt or pepper. Serve at room temperature or chilled.

Variation

Lemony Couscous and Vegetable Salad

Replace the vinegar with an equal amount of lemon juice.

COOKING TIME:
2 minutes

PREP TIME:
25 minutes

SERVES: *4*

EQUIPMENT:
liquid measuring cup, small microwave-safe mug or bowl, microwave, measuring cups and spoons, large bowl, fork, all-purpose knife, cutting board, vegetable peeler, small bowl

Cheap Tip

Avoid buying fresh herbs like basil or parsley in plastic packages; all you're paying for is the packaging and a small amount of the herb (which won't be that fresh to start with). If possible, buy herbs at a farmers market or an ethnic market, where they're much cheaper.

Desserts

Still have room for dessert? We hope so, because we've lined up a host of decadent goodies that are guaranteed to keep your sweet tooth happy. Even better, you won't need any specialized baking equipment or expert know-how to make them.

In all of the other chapters, we've encouraged you to vary the recipes according to your tastes. With dessert recipes, however, there's not as much room to experiment. Changing an ingredient can throw off the entire recipe. And when you go off-recipe too much, there's no guarantee that it will still work. If you want to make substantial changes, such as incorporating whole grains or reducing the amount of fat, consult a baking cookbook with recipes developed specifically for that purpose.

If you feel intimidated at the thought of making baked goods, don't sweat it. Sometimes the most impressive desserts are the simplest ones, such as a bowl of fresh fruit with a squeeze of lime juice, a dish of ice cream doused in a shot of espresso or strong coffee, or our favorite: a big hunk of quality chocolate.

Dark Chocolate Sauce

Chocolate and cream—that's all it takes to make a great chocolate sauce. Served warm or cold, this decadent sauce is perfect for drizzling over ice cream.

PREP TIME:
3 minutes

COOKING TIME:
2 minutes

Makes 1 1/4 cups (300 ml) sauce

EQUIPMENT:
liquid measuring cup, medium microwave-safe bowl, microwave, measuring cups, spoon

3/4 cup (180 ml) heavy cream or whipping cream
1 cup (6 ounces/170 g) semisweet chocolate chips (see Cheap Tip)

1. Place the cream in a medium microwave-safe bowl and microwave on high until it is steaming hot. (Stop the microwave every 30 seconds to check on the cream.)
2. Add the chocolate chips to the cream and stir until melted and smooth.
3. Serve the sauce warm or chilled. (The sauce will thicken as it cools.)

Variation

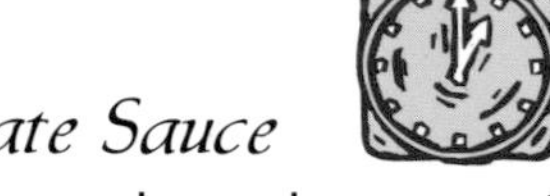

Stovetop Dark Chocolate Sauce

If you don't have a microwave, heat the cream in a small saucepan over medium heat. Place the chocolate chips in a small bowl. Once the cream is hot, pour it over the chocolate chips. Stir until the chocolate is melted and the sauce is smooth.

Cheap Tip

The cheapest and most convenient form of chocolate to use for desserts is semisweet chocolate chips. We like to have them on hand for whenever a chocolate craving hits. If you're a chocoholic and can justify spending a bit more for *primo* chocolate, substitute a good-quality chocolate bar by chopping it into little pieces. Some good brands to look for include Valrhona, Ghirardelli, Lindt, and Scharffen Berger. (They're sold in the candy aisle of the supermarket.) Whatever you do, do not use unsweetened chocolate, such as the chocolate squares sold in the baking section of the supermarket. As the name suggests, this chocolate is very bitter and should only be used in recipes that specifically call for unsweetened chocolate.

Hot Caramel Sauce

This buttery sauce makes a luxurious topping for ice cream and cake. Or, if no one's looking, just eat it straight off the spoon.

1 cup (200 g) packed light or dark brown sugar
1/2 cup (1 stick/100 g) butter
1/3 cup (80 ml) heavy cream or whipping cream
Pinch of salt

1. Place the brown sugar, butter, cream, and salt in a large microwave-safe bowl (see tip).
2. Microwave the mixture on high for 2 minutes. Stir with a fork to combine the ingredients and get out any lumps of brown sugar.
3. Microwave on high for 2 minutes more, or until the caramel sauce is smooth. Serve the sauce hot or at room temperature. (It will thicken as it cools.)

PREP TIME:
1 minute

COOKING TIME:
4 minutes
Makes 1 cup sauce

EQUIPMENT:
measuring cups, liquid measuring cup, large microwave-safe bowl, microwave, fork

Variation

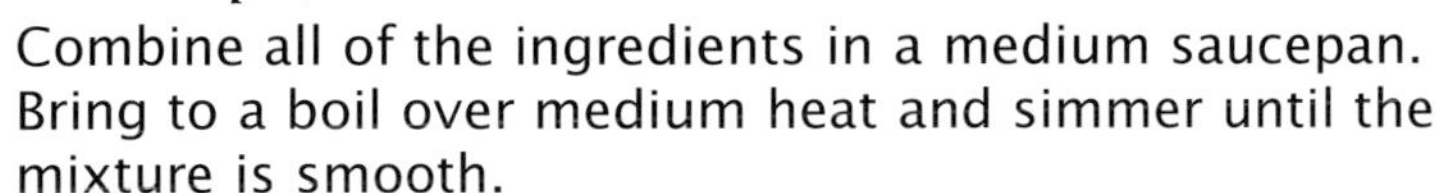

Stovetop Hot Caramel Sauce

Combine all of the ingredients in a medium saucepan. Bring to a boil over medium heat and simmer until the mixture is smooth.

Don't Let This Happen to You

It's important to use a large bowl when you heat the ingredients in the microwave because the mixture bubbles up a lot. If the bowl isn't big enough, the caramel sauce could spill over the sides, making a sticky mess.

The Very Best Chocolate Chip Cookies

This recipe is based on the very best chocolate chip cookie recipe ever, the Nestlé Toll House Chocolate Chip Cookies recipe. We've included the recipe here in case you get a different brand of chocolate chips or buy them from the bulk section.

1 cup (140 g) plus 2 tablespoons all-purpose flour
1/2 teaspoon baking soda
1/2 teaspoon salt
1/2 cup (1 stick/100 g) butter, softened
1/2 cup (100 g) packed light or dark brown sugar
1/3 cup (65 g) sugar
1 large egg
1/2 teaspoon vanilla extract
1 cup (6 ounces/170 g) semisweet chocolate chips
1/2 cup (50 g) chopped walnuts or pecans (optional)

1. Preheat the oven to 375 degrees F (190 degrees C).
2. Combine the flour, baking soda, and salt in a small bowl.
3. In a large bowl, stir the butter, brown sugar, sugar, egg, and vanilla until the mixture is creamy.
4. Add the flour mixture and stir to combine.
5. Stir in the chocolate chips, and nuts if desired.
6. Using a small spoon, drop 12 walnut-sized balls of dough onto the baking sheet, spacing them about 2 inches apart.
7. Bake the cookies for 9 to 11 minutes, or until they are golden. (If your oven heats unevenly, you may want to turn the baking sheet around halfway through the baking time.)
8. Cool the cookies on the baking sheet for 2 minutes, then transfer to a wire rack to cool completely (if they last that long).
9. Repeat Steps 6 to 8 with the rest of the cookie dough. If you are using just one cookie sheet, make sure it has cooled off before you drop the second batch of dough on it or the dough will melt into little puddles.

PREP TIME:
14 minutes

BAKING TIME:
18 to 22 minutes
Makes 24 cookies

EQUIPMENT:
measuring cups and spoons, small bowl, large bowl, large spoon, baking sheet, pancake turner, wire rack

Variation

The Very Best Chocolate Chip Bar Cookies

This version of the recipe is a bit faster because you don't have to divide the batter into individual cookies. Spread the cookie batter into a 9 x 9-inch baking pan or a 13 x 9-inch baking pan. If you're using 9 x 9-inch pan, bake for 18 to 21 minutes, or until golden. If you're using a 13 x 9-inch pan, bake for 12 to 15 minutes. Cool the bar cookies in the pan. Cut into desired number of bar cookies.

Don't Let This Happen to You

Once you put the cookies in the oven, the most important step in the recipe begins. Don't leave the kitchen. If you step away for a few moments, you may come back to find that your wonderful cookies are burned to a crisp. If your oven runs hot or your baking sheet is quite thin, the cookies will bake faster than the recipe says.

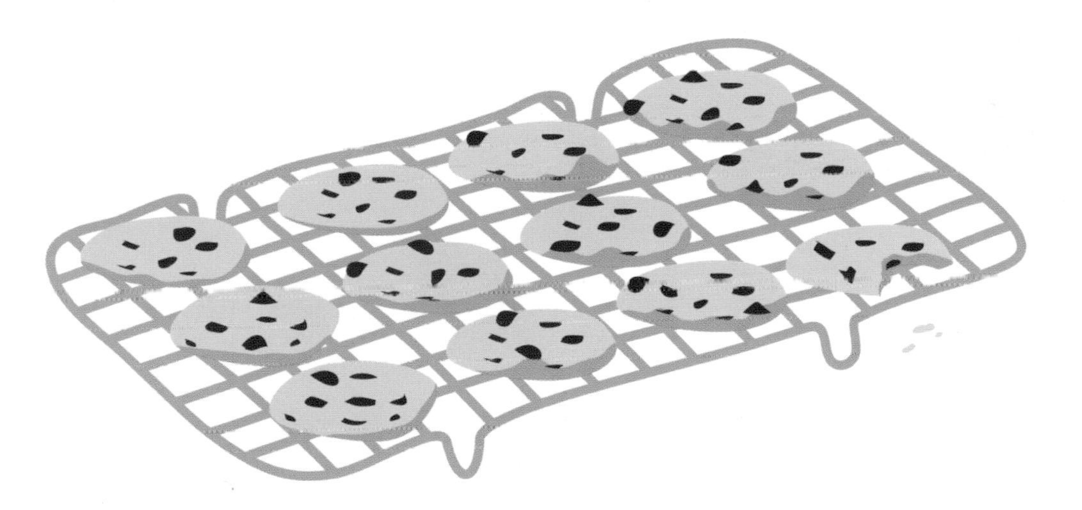

Walnut Chunk Brownies

If you love intense chocolate flavor, these brownies might just be the best you've ever had. We like to serve them warm with vanilla ice cream on top.

1/2 cup (120 ml) vegetable oil
1 cup (200 g) sugar
2 large eggs
1 teaspoon vanilla extract
1/2 cup (70 g) flour
1/3 cup (40 g) unsweetened cocoa powder (such as Hershey's)
Large pinch of salt
1 cup (6 ounces/170 g) semisweet chocolate chips
1/2 cup (50 g) chopped walnuts

1. Preheat the oven to 375 degrees F (190 degrees C).
2. Line the bottom and sides of a 9-inch square baking pan with a sheet of nonstick foil, allowing the foil to hang over the ends by about 2 inches. (If you can't find nonstick foil, use regular aluminum foil greased with 1 teaspoon of vegetable oil.)
3. Place the vegetable oil, sugar, eggs, and vanilla in a large bowl and stir with a fork or whisk until well blended.
4. Add the flour, cocoa, and salt; mix until the flour is incorporated into the batter.
5. Stir in the chocolate chips and walnuts.
6. Pour the batter into the baking pan, using a rubber spatula to scrape out the bowl and smooth the top of the batter.
7. Bake the brownies for 40 to 45 minutes. (If your oven heats unevenly, you may want to turn the baking pan around halfway through the baking time.) The top of the brownies should be crusty and firm rather than soft and squishy.
8. Cool the brownies in the baking pan on a wire rack. Holding the edges of the foil, lift the brownies out of the pan. Cut into 6 to 9 brownies.

PREP TIME:
10 minutes

BAKING TIME:
45 minutes

Makes 6 to 9 brownies

EQUIPMENT:
9-inch square baking pan, nonstick foil, liquid measuring cup, measuring cups and spoons, large bowl, fork or whisk, rubber spatula, wire rack, knife

Variation

Brownies with a Twist

Feel free to run wild with this brownie recipe. Use milk chocolate chips or bittersweet chocolate chips in place of the semisweet chips. You can even use butterscotch chips, toffee bits, chopped-up candy bars, or whatever you like. Or replace the walnuts with pecans or another favorite nut.

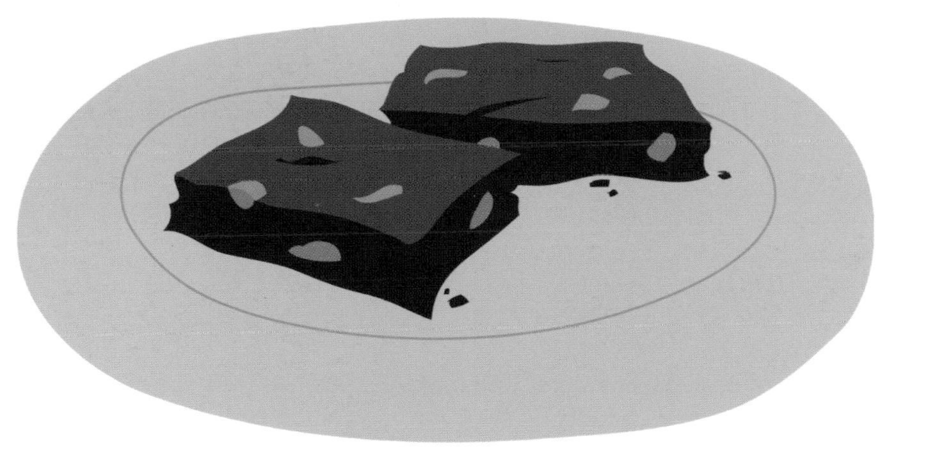

Rich Chocolate Cake with Chocolate Frosting

This recipe makes enough batter for a one-layer cake, enough to share with a couple of friends (or not). To make a double-decker cake, double the cake and frosting recipes.

Measuring ingredients accurately is critical for this recipe, so refresh your knowledge of how to measure by consulting the tips on page 3.

1/3 cup (80 ml) vegetable oil, plus 1 teaspoon to grease the baking pan
1 cup flour (140 g), plus 1 1/2 teaspoons to prepare the baking pan
1 cup (200 g) sugar
2 large eggs
1 cup (240 ml) whole or lowfat milk
1 teaspoon vanilla extract
1/3 cup (40 g) unsweetened cocoa powder (such as Hershey's)
2 teaspoons baking powder
Large pinch of salt
Chocolate frosting (recipe follows)

1. Preheat the oven to 350 degrees F (180 degrees C).
2. Pour 1 teaspoon oil into a 9-inch square or round pan and use your fingers to spread the oil evenly across the bottom and sides. Sprinkle 1 1/2 teaspoons flour in the pan, and tip the pan back and forth to coat the surface with flour. Shake out any excess flour.
3. Place the 1/3 cup (80 ml) oil, sugar, and eggs in a large bowl, stirring with a fork to combine.
4. Add the milk and vanilla and stir to combine.
5. Add the 1 cup (140 g) flour, cocoa, baking powder, and salt; stir to combine.
6. Pour the batter into the greased and floured baking pan, using a rubber spatula to scrape out the bowl and smooth the top of the batter.
7. Bake the cake for 40 to 45 minutes, or until a knife inserted in the center comes out clean. (If your oven heats unevenly, you may want to turn the baking pan around halfway through the baking time.)
8. Let the cake cool completely before topping with the chocolate frosting.

PREP TIME:
20 minutes

BAKING TIME:
40 to 45 minutes

SERVES: *6 to 8*

EQUIPMENT:
measuring cups and spoons, 9-inch square or round baking pan, liquid measuring cup, large bowl, fork, rubber spatula, knife

Chocolate Frosting

The official name for this frosting is "ganache" (pronounced gahn-AHSH), but you just need to know that it's the most versatile frosting/glaze/dessert sauce ever invented. It is superb poured over cake or ice cream and may be used as an easy but elegant dip for strawberries and bananas.

3/4 cup (180 ml) heavy cream or whipping cream
1 cup (6 ounces/170 g) semisweet chocolate chips
1 to 2 tablespoons powdered sugar (optional) (if it's at all lumpy, press out the lumps with the back of a spoon)

1. Place the cream in a small saucepan over medium heat. Warm the cream until it steams, but do not bring to a boil.
2. Place the chocolate chips in a small bowl. Pour the hot cream over the chocolate chips and stir until the chocolate is completely melted.
3. If you like your frosting to be sweeter, add 1 to 2 tablespoons powdered sugar to the chocolate mixture and stir to combine.
4. The chocolate sauce thickens as it cools, which means you can use it as a glaze while it's still warm, or let it cool to room temperature and spread it like a frosting.

PREP TIME:
3 minutes

COOKING TIME:
2 minutes

Makes 1 1/4 cups (300 ml) frosting

EQUIPMENT:
liquid measuring cup, small saucepan, measuring cups and spoons, small bowl, spoon

Variation

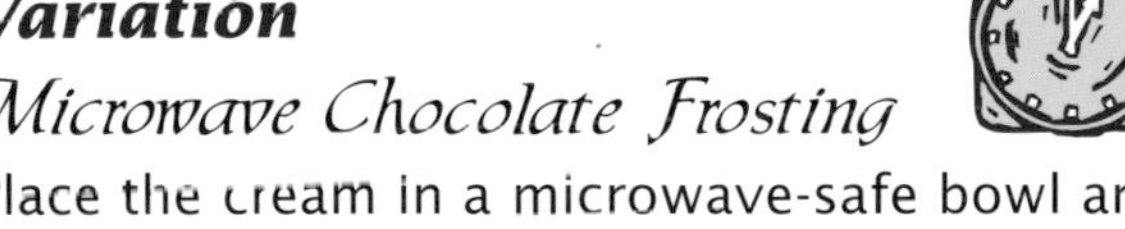

Microwave Chocolate Frosting

Place the cream in a microwave-safe bowl and heat on high for 30 seconds at a time, until the cream is hot. Add the chocolate chips and stir to combine. Stir in the powdered sugar, if desired.

Strawberries with Sour Cream and Brown Sugar

Sour cream sweetened with brown sugar is a super-simple, versatile dessert sauce that can be used with all kinds of fruit, including cherries, peaches, and apricots.

1 pint ripe strawberries (see Cheap Tip)
1 (8 ounce/225 g) container sour cream
2 tablespoons packed light or dark brown sugar
1/2 teaspoon vanilla extract

1. Rinse the strawberries. Cut off the stems, if desired.
2. Place the sour cream, brown sugar, and vanilla in a small bowl. Stir with a fork until well combined.
3. To serve, slice the strawberries in half and drizzle the sauce over them. Or leave the strawberries whole and dip them in the sauce.
4. Any leftover, un-sauced strawberries may be placed in a freezer bag and frozen. (Smoothies, anyone?)

PREP TIME: *5 minutes*

SERVES: *3 to 4*

EQUIPMENT: *paring knife, cutting board, measuring spoons, small bowl, fork*

Cheap Tip

Wait until at least spring to buy strawberries; they're much cheaper and more flavorful then. Check the container first to make sure the strawberries are not moldy, mushy, or underripe. Stay away from any that look pale or green.

Chocolate-Covered Strawberries

Everyone loves strawberries dipped in chocolate, which makes them the perfect thing to serve when you want to impress someone special.

1 pint ripe strawberries
3/4 cup (4 1/2 ounces/125 g) semisweet chocolate chips

1. Rinse the strawberries, leaving the stems on. Dry with paper towels.
2. Place the chocolate chips in a small microwave-safe bowl and microwave on high until they are almost melted. Stop the microwave every 30 seconds to stir and check on them (see tip).
3. Place a sheet of waxed paper on a plate. Holding the strawberries by their stems, dip them in the melted chocolate one by one. Place them on the waxed paper.
4. Refrigerate the strawberries until the chocolate hardens, about 20 minutes.

Don't Let This Happen to You

There are at least two things that can go wrong when you melt chocolate. First of all, chocolate burns easily, especially in the microwave, because it's hard to tell when it's melted. Even if the chocolate is still in the shape of chocolate chips, you have to stir it to be able to tell if it's completely melted. Stop the microwave every 30 seconds to check.

The second thing that can go wrong with chocolate is not so obvious. Believe it or not, one drop of water can ruin an entire batch of melted chocolate by making it stiff, lumpy, and grainy. Pastry chefs call this disaster "seizing up"—you'll know it when you see it. To prevent this problem, make sure that the bowl is completely dry before you add the chocolate chips. Also, don't cover the bowl during or after heating, as condensation may collect and drip into the chocolate. If the chocolate has seized up, stir in a small amount of cream to see if it smoothes out. If that doesn't work, you'll have to start all over again.

PREP TIME:
8 minutes

COOKING TIME:
2 minutes

RESTING TIME:
20 minutes

SERVES: *3 to 4*

EQUIPMENT:
paper towels, measuring cups, small microwave-safe bowl, microwave, spoon, waxed paper, plate

Apple Crisp

Our favorite part of apple crisp is its spicy, crunchy topping, so we pile on plenty of it. Depending on the size of your baking dish, there might be more topping than you can fit on top of the apples. If that's the case, freeze the leftover topping in a freezer bag for the next time you want to bake a fruit crisp.

PREP TIME: *20 minutes*

BAKING TIME: *55 minutes*

SERVES: *4 to 6*

EQUIPMENT: *measuring cups and spoons, large bowl, fork, vegetable peeler, all-purpose knife, cutting board, pie plate or other small baking dish*

3/4 cup (110 g) flour
1/2 cup (100 g) sugar
1/4 cup (20 g) rolled oats
2 teaspoons ground cinnamon
1/2 cup (1 stick/100 g) butter, softened
2 tablespoons chopped almonds or walnuts (optional)
4 medium apples, preferably 2 tart (such as Granny Smith) and 2 sweet (such as Fuji)
Vanilla ice cream

1. Preheat the oven to 350 degrees F (180 degrees C).
2. Place the flour, sugar, rolled oats, and cinnamon in a large bowl, stirring with a fork to combine.
3. Add the butter and mash evenly throughout the flour mixture. The topping should be in large crumbs, not a solid piece of dough. Mix in the nuts, if desired.
4. Peel the apples and cut them in quarters. Cut out the cores. Cut each apple quarter into four slices.
5. Place the apples in a pie plate or other baking dish (see Cheap Tip). Scatter the topping evenly over the apples. Don't worry if the apples peek through the topping; that's the way it should be.
6. Bake the apple crisp for 55 minutes, or until the top is crispy and browned and the apples are tender when pierced with a fork. (If your oven heats unevenly, you may want to turn the baking dish around halfway through the baking time.)
7. Serve the apple crisp warm, if possible, preferably with a scoop of vanilla ice cream.

Variation

Berry Crisp

Substitute 1 to 1 1/2 (16 ounce/455 g) bags of frozen blackberries for the apples. The amount of berries will depend on the size of your baking dish; fill it no more than 2/3 full, as the berry juices have a tendency to bubble up and over the sides. Toss the berries with 2 tablespoons of sugar and 1 tablespoon of cornstarch before placing them in the baking dish.

Cheap Tip

We like to save and reuse those handy disposable aluminum pie plates that come with frozen pie crusts and pies sold at pie restaurants. If you don't own a pie plate, don't go out and buy one just for the sake of making this recipe. Apple crisp is so free-form that it readily adapts itself to any type of small baking dish. For instance, if you have a 9-inch square baking dish, use that instead. The baking time will be about the same.

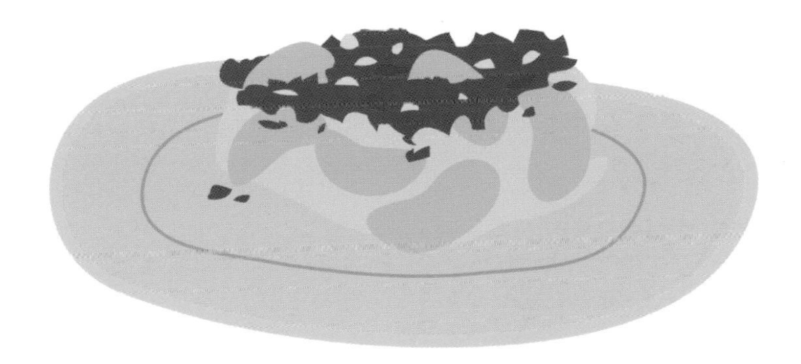

Easy Pumpkin Pie

Baking a pie is much easier than you'd think. Keep things simple by using a frozen pie crust—the kind that comes in its own baking pan.

1 (15 ounce/425 g) can pure pumpkin (not pumpkin pie filling)
1/2 cup (100 g) sugar
1/3 cup (70 g) packed light or dark brown sugar
1 1/2 teaspoons ground cinnamon (see Cheap Tip)
3/4 teaspoon ground ginger
1/4 teaspoon ground cloves
2 large eggs, beaten with a fork
1 1/4 cups (300 ml) whole milk
1 frozen deep-dish pie crust (no need to thaw)

1. Preheat the oven to 350 degrees F (180 degrees C).
2. Scoop the canned pumpkin into a medium bowl. Add the sugar, brown sugar, cinnamon, ginger, and cloves and stir with a fork until well blended.
3. Add the eggs and milk and stir until smooth.
4. Pour the pumpkin mixture into the unbaked pie crust. Place the pie pan on top of a baking sheet.
5. Bake the pie for 65 minutes, or until the center no longer jiggles. (If your oven heats unevenly, you may want to turn the pie around halfway through the baking time.) When you stick a knife into the pie, it should come out clean.
6. Let the pie cool completely on a wire rack. Serve chilled or at room temperature. Refrigerate any leftovers.

PREP TIME:
12 minutes

BAKING TIME:
65 minutes

SERVES: *8*

EQUIPMENT:
can opener, rubber spatula, medium bowl, measuring cups and spoons, fork, liquid measuring cup, baking sheet, knife, wire rack

Cheap Tip

We've said it before, but it bears repeating: Buy spices from the bulk section of a health-food store, only as much as you need. Otherwise they'll be haunting your cupboard for years to come.

Index

C

D

E

T

U

V

W

Y